THE DEEP SEA CANOE

THE STORY OF THIRD WORLD MISSIONARIES
IN THE SOUTH PACIFIC

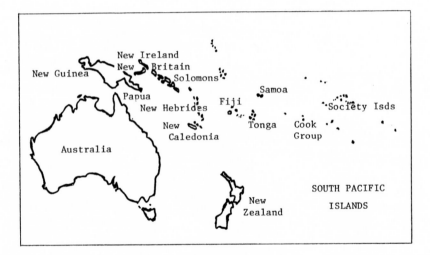

Fig. 1 Map of the South Pacific

THE DEEP SEA CANOE

THE STORY OF THIRD WORLD MISSIONARIES IN THE SOUTH PACIFIC

ALAN R. TIPPETT

William Carey Library
Pasadena, California
www.WCLBooks.com

Publisher's Note: The first edition of this book was prepared from a camera-ready copy created and edited by the late author, Alan Tippett. For this reprint, we have updated the title page, copyright page, and About the Author page, as well as the cover, but have left the main text as in the original.

Cover design: Chris Kim

Published by William Carey Library
1605 E. Elizabeth Street, Pasadena, California 91104
www.WCLBooks.com

William Carey Library is a ministry of the U.S. Center for World Mission, Pasadena, California.

Library of Congress Cataloging in Publication Data
Tippett, Alan Richard.
The deep-sea canoe.
ISBN 0-87808-158-5
1. Missions--Oceanica. I. Title.
BV3670.T57   266'.0099   77-8660

Printed in the United States of America

THE DEEP-SEA CANOE

is dedicated to

the treasured memory of

my companions of

the Road

and the Deep

Kiniwiliame Namoumou
Elimi Kurusiga
Setareki Rika
Etuate Sokiveta
Iliesa Senikau

Contents

Illustrations

Preface:
The Deep-Sea Canoe

THE DEEP-SEA CANOE is a symbol from the South Pacific
World. A century and a half ago, Fijian and Tongan deep-sea
canoes plied from island to island with trade, warriors and
tribute. More often than not their narratives were woven into the cultural configuration of cannibalism and war. These
included double canoes *(drua)*, sometimes called "sacred canoes" because war and cannibalism were religiously institution-
alized. Some of these were longer than Captain Cook's *Endeav-
our*. There were other deep-sea craft - the *tabilai* and the
camakau - which may still be found in the outer islands today.

In the first half of the 19th Century a dramatic
change took place. The use of the deep-sea canoe steadily
shifted from the business of war and cannibalism to the transport of missionaries from one island group to another. These
men were Tahitians, Tongans and Fijians. They spread the
Gospel message beyond their own reefs right across the Pacific. They made phenomenal voyages between groups hundreds of
miles apart, with remarkable skill in navigation. Joeli Bulu,
Joni Havea, Juliasa Naulivou, Sailasa Faone, Wesele Lagi and
Jeremaia Latu, all Tongan missionaries to Fiji before 1840,
sailed over that 500 miles by deep-sea canoe.

Some of the British missionaries used this form of
navigation. Thomas Williams in particular, used a canoe
named *Kurabui* for his inter-insular visitation in the following decade. The canoe became a symbol for missionary expansion. In Fiji we are talking of a deep-sea canoe - a *drua*,
a *camakau* or a *tabilai*, not a light-draught canoe without a
proper deck, that is poled to and fro in the rivers and within the reefs *(takia)*. True, many town Fijians who have been

educated for the urban rather than the nautical life, and
some inland islanders, call any canoe a takia. But the whole
point of this quite indigenous concept is that the missionary
symbol is a deep-sea canoe. There is to be no enclosure of
their Church within the reefs. The island churches found
themselves compelled to reach out beyond the reefs, and that
could not be done in a light-draught canoe. In my years in
Kadavu I often did my own missionary itineration in a deep-
sea canoe, and many times in bad weather have I been close to
disaster that I am fully aware of the significance of the deep-
sea descriptor.

There is a record of Joeli Bulu borrowing a large deep-
sea canoe, named *Kinikinilau*, from Ratu Cakobau, in 1869, to
visit the island of Nairai. They ran into a hurricane and
blinding rain. The canoe rolled and plunged so violently
that her fastenings were endangered, and the sailyard was
jerked from its place on the bow and fell into the sea. They
tugged and strained until they got it in its place again, but
many of the company having given up hope, they had to lower the
sail and let the storm carry them by its own force, without a
sail. They lashed the sail to the deck, and Stephen, a Lasa-
kauan, called the company to prayer, leading first himself and
then asking Joeli to follow.

No sooner had the prayer ended than the storm subsided
"not growing weaker, and ceasing gradually, but suddenly, in
a moment. And there was a calm." [I quote Joeli's actual
words]. They began to secure their parted fastenings and headed for an island that had appeared in their course, and skull-
ed for land. As they did so the storm began again and they
hoisted the sail. The wind grew stronger and stronger.   A
cable parted and they lost an anchor, but they were able to
enter the passage through the reef, and with some difficulty
managed to beach the canoe; by which time the hurricane was
blowing full force again from the opposite direction.   Although many trees and houses fell, they were able to "sing
praises to God for his wonderful goodness" as Joeli put it.
Anyone who is familiar with the circular pattern of this kind
of Fijian weather disturbance will know the canoe had crossed
"the eye of the hurricane".

These Fijian and Tongan missionaries could boast with
Paul of suffering shipwreck, of spending days and nights in
the deep, and journeying in the perils of the sea, of weari-
ness, of cold and of watching (II Cor 11:25ff.). And as much
as any western missionaries they were responsible for the
spread of the Church across the South Pacific.

Seventeen years of deliberate indigenizing phased out the old colonial type of mission in Fiji. This transitional period terminated in 1964 with the inauguration of the now completely autonomous Conference. One of the rituals of the public festivities was the presentation of a model deep-sea canoe by the highest Chiefs of the land to the Church, as a symbolic reminder of their missionary commission. The first President of the Conference was installed into office by being clothed with the official presidential stole. This beautiful vestment carries two symbols - the symbol of the Faith, the cross, which is a reminder of the power of the Gospel, and a Fijian deep-sea canoe, a cultural symbol of the commission to go forth with that Gospel beyond the reefs.

This little book is an attempt to recapture something of the missionary heritage of the island people themselves, and put it in a biblical frame of reference. It is not a documented history (although it could well have been so) but is rather a simply written account for the young Christians of the Islands today, so that they may know the history of how they came by grace to their present position in the Christian Faith.

1

Mission Under God

Almighty God, who didst send Thy light on the
heathen through Jesus Christ the true light;
drive the dark out of our hearts with Thy Word
and Thy Spirit; shine on our islands with the
light of everlasting life, that they may know
their sin, and may believe in Jesus the Saviour;
that they may find love and peace, and fighting
and heathen ways may pass away, that they may
all come to Thee repenting and believing, following with all their hearts Thy rule; through
Jesus Christ our Lord. *Amen.*

> Prayer of Bishop Patteson
> from the Melanesian Brotherhood's
> *Morning and Evening Prayers*

We travelled along the coast of Malaita with two Melanesian Brothers. They left our company at a place from which a
trail led inland into the mountains, where the people had not
yet accepted Christ. These mountaineers were enemies of the
saltwater people. They had trade relations, but their market
was carried out between two rows of hostile warriors. Yet the
Brotherhood felt *the times were ripe*. The mountain villages
were coming to Christ, forming congregations and providing
pastoral nurture. Then the Brothers would depart and move on
deeper into the pagan region.

1

In the record of Christian missions down through the centuries we come across periods of remarkable vigour when the pioneering bands have penetrated new lands and planted Christian communities across the countryside. It was like this in the 1st Century, as has been recorded in the *Acts of the Apostles*. It was the same in the narrative of how the Gospel spread in Britain, and in Ireland and in Germany. However much legend has come to surround the records of Augustine, Patrick and Boniface, one thing we know – those medieval movements from animism to Christianity were the most dramatic and significant changes of faith position those people had known, and took possession of communities of people whole. They changed the course of history.

In this little book I shall narrate some of the more recent (and still documentable) events of the Christian movement in the Central South Pacific, bringing the focus not on the western missionary figures (whose presence admittedly was quite real, nevertheless), but on the South Pacific islanders themselves, in as much as they were engaged in the missionary penetration, the uprooting of animism, the substitution of Christianity and the planting of the Church. We will see how the island people themselves, once they discovered the power of the Gospel were enabled to bear persecution, to triumph in encounter with the powers of their past, and became so obsessed with the evangel that they could not rest until they had claimed their homelands for Christ. This is, therefore, a book about Third World missionaries during the 19th Century.

The modern period of Protestant missions may be said to have begun in the last decade of the 18th Century with the activities of William Carey and (as far as the Pacific was concerned) with the formation of the London Missionary Society (LMS), whose missionaries penetrated Tahiti and the surrounding islands. From the island converts of this mission, and particularly from Raiatea, came a band of men who went forth with apostolic zeal to win the Polynesian islands to the west for Christ.

Another similar British body to the LMS was the Wesleyan Missionary Society (WMS) whose missionaries operated in Tonga, Fiji and New Zealand. The two missions met in Samoa. The triumph of the Gospel in Tonga led to the missionary penetration of Fiji; and eventually Fijians and Tongans (some Samoans and Rotumans) carried the Gospel further westwards to New Britain and New Ireland, and subsequently to Papua, the Solomon Islands and North Australia. The Tahitian missionaries also penetrated Melanesia. Many of these Third World missionaries were 'faithful unto death' and their graves are found in foreign soil of islands that are now Christian.

The origins of these indigenous missionary movements must be traced back theologically to the Evangelical Revival in Britain. Sometime later the Churches which emerged through this movement received the missionary commission. The Wesleyan movement and that of Whitefield ultimately gave us the WMS and LMS, and from the evangelical party in the Church of England we had the Church Missionary Society (CMS) which also operated with the Maoris in New Zealand. When you pick up a hymnbook and sing the compositions of Wesley, Watts and Toplady, for example, you are drawing from the three wings of this movement, the effects of which reached the Pacific between 1796 and the mid-19th Century. It is this period and penetration which is considered in this book - more particularly the role of the islander himself in it. The South Pacific island convert found the theology of John Wesley quite congenial, and no historian can escape the evidence that the experiences of the Evangelical Revival were truly echoed in the South Pacific Islands.

Times were innovative in Britain. The country was passing through a period of major social change, like Suva and Port Moresby today. There were new kinds of roads and transport, new dimensions in engineering, and everywhere there was experiment. More money was available for investment and Christain people were ready to use this in the Lord's work. They supported the new missionary societies and also the "horizontal structures" like the British and Foreign Bible Society (BFBS) and Religious Tract Society (RTS) which they considered part of their missionary thrust in the world. Education also was developing and experimental.

It was also a time of new discoveries outside of England because of navigation. Sailors explored new oceans, and returned home with tales of people who had strange customs and spoke unknown languages. Captain Cook had explored the Pacific. His reports were printed in England. Carey read them and asked the question - "We have found new seas and new races of people who have never heard of Christ: What does this mean to Christian people to whom God has committed the Gospel in our day? What does the Great Commission mean for the English evangelicals in 1792?" It was out of this question that the notion of modern missionary responsibility arose in Britain and that British missionaries found themselves sent after the apostolic pattern to the South Pacific by the home churches which supported the LMS, WMS and CMS. The distribution of these activities over the South Pacific may be seen on the accompanying map.

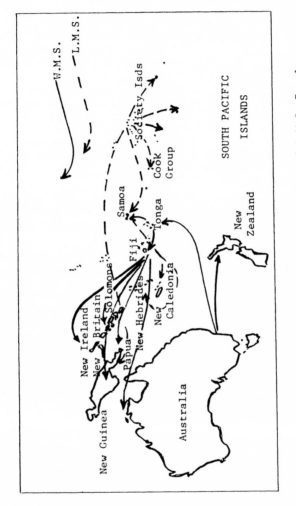

Fig. 3 Showing the Diffusion of the W.M.S. and L.M.S. People Movements Across the South Pacific Ocean

That is how the British missionaries came to be in the
Pacific: but this is not a book about them so much as about
their South Pacific co-workers. The task of collecting the
material for this narrative was not an easy one. Nearly all
the books about Pacific missions were printed in England,
Australia or America, for Christian readers of those countries.
They were the people who sent the missionaries, forwarded medical supplies and educational materials, built the missionary
ship, paid for the printing of Bibles in the vernacular languages and so on. They wanted to know how their missionaries
were getting on, so it was expected that books would focus on
these men and women rather than on their South Pacific co-
workers. So very little has been written about the island
evangelists, and their tremendously important role is often
overlooked. Neither is it easy to recapture these narratives
of their exploits today. This is a tragedy because much of
the pioneering missionary thrust was actually the work of islanders, not of westerners.

However, when one reads the letters written by the
early western missionaries to friends of the family, their
notebooks and diaries, and their reports in the church records,
one will discover that they wrote much about the good work of
their island colleagues. One will also be impressed by the
dependence of the western missionary on his faithful island
offsider. This is especially so of those who worked with
Fijians and Tongans. (I am sure I would find the same in other
places if I had access to the records.) I have given a good
many years of my life looking for these letters and diaries,
and many of the episodes in this little book have come from
such unprinted documents. Therefore, one reason for my writing this present account is to set the record straight and
stress an important point not sufficiently emphasized in the
more promotional histories of mission. The Christian mission
in the South Pacific down to the colonial period was more an
indigenous than a foreign mission.

Another thing I want to say is that I myself have a
great debt to my Fijian colleagues in a later generation from
that of the pioneers. It is true that I gave myself wholly
to the Fijian people, but from them I received far more. I
found them still very like the Old Testament people - living
communally in a subsistance society, with their life of agricultural activity interwoven with their church experiences.
The Old Testament became a new world to me after experiencing
life lived close to the soil with these people. Furthermore,
I learned much of the communal life. I discovered how western
an individualist I was, and koinonia became a new reality. I
also discovered the dynamic of what I shall call in this book

"power encounter" - how a Christian faces a force of evil in
the power and authority of Christ - and here the Scriptures
again become more meaningful.

This meant a whole reorientation of my own religious
life, without which this little book could not have been written. History, anthropology and theology are interwoven in
its pages. Life is like that. It really cannot be compart-
mentalized.

The history might have been put together in the formal
style of a classical history, and documented; but as I am
writing for an island audience that their heritage be not forgotten I have tried to be not over academic. For the same
reason I want it to be culturally relevant - I try to forget
my personal ethnic background and write in the style of my
own cross-cultural experiences in the islands. Theological
it certainly is, because it was a cross-cultural application
of a biblical commission (Mt 28:18-20) that inspired the mission
to the South Pacific. My hope is that the three ingredients
will be interwoven in each chapter, and that a younger generation of South Pacific islanders, to whom I have dedicated this
book, will discover a biblical theology of mission which was
actually worked out historically in their own islands, and
thereby discover its dynamic for themselves.

. . . .

The title I have given this chapter is "Mission Under
God." The phrase reminds us that we are not recording merely
human history, we are not just dependent on our own skills.
It is not our work. It is God's work. He is in control, and
we are trying to do what He wants us to do. Of course, if
He appoints us to be stewards He expects us to be faithful,
and if we are not faithful and obedient to Him things will
not go right. But basically everything depends on God. He
protects us, He guides us, He gives us blessing in the work,
and as I read the history of the growing of the Church in the
South Pacific it seems to me I just cannot explain it without
God. There are some historians who say that history is only
a "biography of great men," but the history of the planting
and growth of the Church is the story of God at work, and I
must start at this point. As we go through this series of
studies we will consider many things that can stop the work.
But the thing that grows, grows because of God.

Now, there are two important doctrines here. One is the
doctrine of *Providence* - God keeping care, directing, always
knowing us and what our problems are, and leading us through
to the place He wants us to go. The other doctrine is *Prevenient Grace* - the "grace that goes before," God going in

front of us and preparing the way, even when we don't know
Him. John Wesley called this "seconding the motion of the
Holy Spirit," that is, the Holy Spirit starting something and
then we ourselves going on, doing what He has prepared the
way for us to do.

Anthropologists have observed human societies going
through change. One kind of change that we are concerned with
is the conversion of people to Christianity. The anthropologist tells us that before a people makes a great social
change in their way of life there is a period of "getting
ready" for that change, that people became "ripe for change,"
so we speak of a cultural "ripeness". The psychologist says
the same thing, that there is a "psychological moment" that is
appropriate for change. Both of these recognize a fact but
neither of them allows for the part that God plays in that
fact.

It is God who prepares the people and "ripens the field
for harvest." We may cultivate. We may plant. We may weed.
But it is God who sends the rain. It is God who gives the
seed and the harvest, and the phrase "fields ripe unto harvest" is a Bible phrase for evangelists.

We are studying God's time when something should happen.
We have it in the New Testament - "in the fulness of time" ,
God sent forth His Son into the world." The Lord did not come
in the days of Babylon, or of Abraham. He used other spokesmen in those times, but he came at that time in Roman history
when there were Roman roads and a universal Greek language,
and when Hebrew ideals were diffused over the Roman world. It
was a perfect time for the spread of the Gospel. So here we
have God working before an evangelist had ever gone into the
place, preparing the way.

Do you remember that passage in the Old Testament which
speaks of Cyrus the King of Persia? I remember, as a young
being very much struck by that reference. The Lord's message
to Cyrus runs something like this - "I have girded thee though
thou hast not known me." And then he goes on to tell how the
gates of brass are going to fall down before the King and the
Jews are going to be released from Babylon. Here is God working in history. Even if people do not know Him, He is at work.

Every now and again somebody (it may be you; it may be
me) gets into that stream of God's will even though he may not
know much about it. God puts His hand on him because He wants
him for a special task. To recognize that God is speaking to
you and to be obedient to His will is very important in Christian mission. In 30 years of studying the history of the

Church in the Pacific it has become clear to me that God
brings situations and people together. God knew the whole
Pacific and He persistently brought people together. When
men responded to His guiding in this way He used them with
mighty power. Many things that happened in the planting of
the Church in the Pacific can only be explained by this kind
of theology.

Take the case of John Williams who built a boat, *The
Messenger of Peace*. He sailed over the sea from Raiatea to
Tonga, and while in Tonga he had fully intended to go to Fiji,
but the Lord stopped him; as he stopped Paul from going up
into Galatia. God was saying to Paul, "I want you to go into
Europe." John Williams was an LMS missionary and he was going
to Tonga en route to Fiji, but the Lord wanted the Tongans to
bring Fiji to Christ. When John Williams arrived in Tonga
the Great Awakening had begun and people were becoming Christian in hundreds. Among those who were' converted was Fouia, a
Samoan, who had come to Tonga by canoe and being caught in the
winds was left there, stranded. This man was converted. As
soon as he was converted he said, "I want this gospel for my
people." Therefore, when Williams came with a boat and some
teachers from Tahiti the Samoan said, "You come over to my
land, I'll open a door for you." And he succeeded in persuad-
ing John Williams to go to Samoa instead of Fiji because Williams recognized that God was in this. He had no way of getting into Fiji. God opened the way into Samoa. So they
boarded *The Messenger of Peace* and sailed to Samoa.

And Fouia said to Williams, "There is one obstacle we
will have to face when we reach Samoa. The High Priest of the
pagan religion will be our enemy and will try to stop us." So
they prayed about this on their way to Samoa, and when they
arrived word came to the boat from the shore that a week earlier the High Priest had died, and there was no High Priest in
Samoa at the time. You can say it was a "psychological moment,"
you can say it was a "cultural moment," but surely God was in
that situation somewhere.

When they reached the shore, Fouia was an attraction because years before he had gone away and the people thought he
was lost, and now they were happy because he had come home.
He had come back a prosperous man. He was in a white man's
ship. He had a white man as a friend, and everybody wanted to
hear what had happened to him while he had been away, and so
he was able to witness. Everyone wanted to listen. Do you
see the way God brought all those different incidents together?
Who turned John Williams away from Fiji to go to Samoa? Who
provided Fouia, the Samoan who was converted in Tonga, as a
spokesman? Who directed that ship to Samoa at precisely the

time they had no High Priest? Who opened the door to the converted Samoan to witness to his friends who thought he was lost? I believe the Lord was in this.

I also want to point out in passing that the evangelist who led those people to Christ was not the white missionary. God had helped build the ship. God had helped that homemade ship to sail 3,000 miles across the ocean. God had made the missionary the coordinator, but He had made the Samoan the evangelist. There are literally hundreds of stories like this.

Let me mention the case of Tanre. He came from the Micronesian islands up in the northern part of the South Pacific and lived there in the days of the Pacific slave trade. Tanre was a sorcerer. He used black magic to kill people, and he had killed a man of the islands. As a result the people of the village were angry and they resolved to retaliate by killing the sorcerer. In great fear Tanre ran away, and met a white man's ship - a bad ship, a slaving ship. In order to save his own life he allowed the slavers to use him as a decoy for the enslavement of unwary islanders. And in this company he fell from bad to worse. The captain of the slaver said that after "so many moons" he would take him back to his island when his people had forgotten the trouble he had caused. But, when the time came for him to go back, his island was hundreds of miles away, so the slaver put him down on the first island he came to.

Now this island had only just become Christian, so Tanre found himself living in a Christian village. The people behaved in a different way from what he expected. They loved God and they loved one another. They helped each other. This was such a new way of life that he began to ask about it. They told him the story of the Saviour, and Tanre repented of his past, and asked, "How can I make restitution for the evil that I have done, first in my own island and then in all these islands? I can only do it by going back to my own island again and giving them this 'good news' that I have heard."

Then quite unexpectedly God sent along another ship that was going that very way, and this ship took Tanre back to his island, the island of Beru, in the Gilberts. At first Tanre's people did not want to listen to him because they knew he had been a sorcerer, but when they heard the story of the place where he had found the Lord, they began to ask for more information. In this way Tanre, the sorcerer and slaver, became a witness for Christ and an evangelist in his own island. That island is entirely Christian today.

Did you ever hear of such a wonderful God who could take a sorcerer and a slaver and make an evangelist out of him? The

Lord did that with John Newton too. Newton was the man who
wrote the hymns, "Amazing Grace" and "How Sweet the Name of
Jesus Sounds." There are many aspects of Christian belief
and theology in these stories. They are stories of sinners
repenting, of trying to make restitution for the evil that
they had done, stories of sinners becoming gospel preachers.
This is the story of salvation because God is striving with
men. There is important doctrine here of God working all the
time (Jn 5: 17), bringing people who do not know Him into the
stream of His will for the purposes of the Gospel.

Let me tell you the story of a witness, a boy called
Benjamin. There are about 280 islands in the Fiji Group, and
it was on one of the biggest of these islands that this happened. The missionary, John Hunt, was sailing in his boat
along the coast. It was actually a boat belonging to the people of another island called Viwa. It was nighttime and they
were looking for shelter. The people along this coast were
the enemies of Viwa, and John Hunt said to the sailors from
Viwa, "Something tells me (or was it Someone?) that we ought
to go to that little village there." And John Hunt later
wrote in his diary, "I don't know why I said that, because I
knew they were enemies." Later on he knew the Lord was in
this. In that village he found a boy who was very sick with
leprosy. He spoke to the boy, and he persuaded the people to
let him take the sick boy away to his mission station for medical care the next morning. When the enemies of Viwa heard
this they said, "Alright, you can take him." They were thinking only that he would get some medical treatment, but of
course this enabled the Viwa canoe to go home safely.

But the young boy not only got medical treatment, he
also heard the Gospel and became very enthusiastic about the
word of truth in the Scriptures. Before long, the disease
became much worse and the missionary knew that the boy was
dying. However, he certainly absorbed a great deal of the
Gospel in the few days that he was there.

Just at this time there arrived a war canoe from another
part of Fiji, and this was under a war chief named Lua. Lua
said to the missionary, "I have heard that you have some 'good
news'. I want a teacher to take back with me to my part of
Fiji to tell us this good news." Hunt replied, "Alas! we have
no one to send." All his preachers were out missioning. Then
the chief, Lua, saw the sick boy, who now had the Christian
name Benjamin. And Benjamin said, "Let me go with Lua."

It takes several days by fast canoe to go from Viwa to
Nadroga where Lua came from, and on that voyage Benjamin told
Lua all he knew of the Gospel. He told him of Christ and his

work, and he told him all the Bible stories he could remember.
Then just as they came in sight of the harbor of the pagan
chief poor Benjamin died. And Lua went into his village, and
all of the Gospel he knew was that which he had learned from
Benjamin. He told the people he wanted them to build a church.
So they built a church. Then Lua said, "I will tell you of
Christ and his work and Benjamin's gospel stories until such
a time as we can have a teacher."

That is how Nadroga opened for the Gospel. And when I
first went down to Fiji I lived just two or three miles from
the site where that canoe landed. I used to go there with my
wife and my two little girls and sometimes have a picnic on
the beach at that spot. If that had been 150 years earlier I
would have been put in a cannibal oven! But now it is a Christian place.

Now, there wasn't any human planning in this. Why did
John Hunt go that night to that particular pagan village?
Who brought Hunt and the leper boy together? Who made him so
receptive to the Gospel? Who brought the chief, Lua, to him
just at that moment before Benjamin died? Who made Lua responsive, and opened up the way to the Church? There are hundreds of stories like this and they all tell the same thing -
that God was in charge. These poor island people who had, as
yet, no education at all were surely the servants of God. It
doesn't matter what our preparation is, if we get into the
current of the will of God He will use us.

On one occasion in Fiji I went up into the mountains.
I was on foot, and overnight there was a heavy rainstorm. When
I came down the mountainside I knew that the river was in flood
and I had no way of crossing but to swim over that stream.
Directly opposite me there was a path, that was my goal, and
so I started to swim. As I swam (and I swam fairly strongly),
the current of the water carried me downstream and eventually
I had to grasp a clump of bamboos about four or five hundred
yards down the river. You see, there were two forces there,
my force, going ahead to reach that goal, and the current
carrying me down to some place I did not want to go. It is
like that when you get into the current of God's will. You
might feel that you have your goal before you. You strive to
meet your goal and you are faithful in your striving. But
there is another force that is carrying you somewhere else
into new areas that you didn't expect. The man who gets out
into the missionary world with God never really knows where he
is going, because his own plans are always subject to change.
And yet I thank the Lord, as I look back over my missionary
life, that time after time He has pushed me into things I did

not intend to do, and I have always come to the conclusion that He knew better than I did.

So let this introduction to our study remind us that it is a narrative of *Mission Under God*. He was bringing about His purposes through the South Sea Island people, without whose assistance the missionaries could have done little. And "Mission Under God" implies two basic theological ideas - the idea of Providence and the idea of Prevenient Grace - God in control and caring for us, and God going before and preparing the way. What a wonderful thing it is to be in the times and purposes of God - the God who acts in history in "the fulness of time" - as servants of the Lord.

Even the Lord himself was under the limitations of time. So he spoke of his time being "not yet come" (Jn 2:4; 7:8). Indeed, in John's Gospel we frequently meet this mode of speech - his (or her) "hour" (7:30; 8:20; 13:1; 16:21) or "the hour is come" (17:1). All of this indicates a divine will behind the drama. Furthermore, the incarnation of our Lord was set in time as God saw it, when "the fulness of the time was come" (Gal 4:4). In the same phrase we are told that all things will be gathered together to the cosmic Christ (Eph 1:10). His death for sinners also was "in due time" (Rom 5:6). This is the biblical view of God in history.

> God, who at sundry times and in divers manners spake in time past unto the fathers by the prophets, hath in these last days spoken unto us by His Son.

This we read in the *Letter to the Hebrews* (1:1-2), which is a record of the work of God in history, that ends by expressing the expectation that the readers of the letter, under God, will be made "perfect in every good work to do His will" (13:20-21). There is, of course, a human role in the history of mission, but the mission is nevertheless "under God," in his providence and grace and in terms of His promises and will.

2

The Missionary Call

In the first chapter we discussed God's providence and grace working in the missionary situation even before the missionaries arrived. We were thinking of God's activity within the missionary program and of how He prepared the way for the coming of the Gospel. This was the divine aspect of the Christian mission. In this chapter I want to look at the other side of the story, because God does not work alone, He works through men and women - the people whom He calls to His ministry and mission as His co-workers. "Co-worker" is a Bible phrase. We are co-workers with God, but we are only co-workers with Him, because He chooses us and *calls* us. So our subject in this study is the *missionary call*.

This is like the work of a farm. When I first put these thoughts together I was in Korea. I had just made a journey on one of the country roads to have a look at the countryside. I noticed that the little valleys which opened out on to the highway were filled with rice fields. As I looked I saw that these beautiful fields were very different from the forest. In the forest everything grew together in a dense mass, but the rice fields were orderly and planned, and had pretty curves of cultivation. I knew immediately that people had been working there. These rice fields didn't come into being by accident. They were planned and planted. Whenever I look at a rice field or vineyard, or a taro patch I remember that God and men are working there together. Of course we know that there couldn't be a harvest if God didn't give it to us. But, on the other hand, it is a wonderful thing to know that he uses men to cultivate the fields and to bring about His purposes. So now in this story of the South Pacific we are going to move on from the work of God to the part that man plays when God calls him as His co-worker.

A short time ago, I saw a newspaper from Australia which reported a fight between two groups of Australian aborigines, and a young man had come out and had run between those two warring parties. He had held up his arms and shouted to them that this was not the way to settle their quarrels. "Listen to me," he said, "I have a better way of settling this disagreement." Then he pleaded with them to stop fighting, until eventually he succeeded in his purpose, and he was able to reconcile the two hostile parties. Now, that was a very brave act and the newspaper reported it because of its bravery. But the newspaper did not tell who the young man was. That young man who had stopped the fight was a Fijian. Now, what was a Fijian doing up there in North Australia among the Australian aborigines whose language was so different from his own? Why was he there? The newspaper did not report that the peacemaker was there as a missionary. The people of his own country and his own home church had sent him to North Australia. If the secular newspaper had given us the full account, it would have told us how, and why, he was able to reconcile those two groups, because he told them that the way of Jesus was a different way from that which they were following. Furthermore, the Lord had called this young Fijian from the very place where the leper boy had been taken, in the story I told you in the first chapter, and the gospel he had preached to Lua, the chief, and the church which had grown in that locality had sent this young man to be a missionary. But the young man himself wanted to be a missionary because God had called him. The name that he had been given as a baby was "Lotu", and *lotu* means "church". So his name was Daniel Church. He told me once that he often thought about why he had that name and God said to him, "I gave you that name because I want you to plant my church in another land." And Daniel had been faithful to his heavenly vision. God had called him, and he went to the mission field. Now, let us think for a few moments about this idea of God's call.

God calls men in many ways, and if we read the Bible we will find that the call comes to different people in different ways. The work that God calls me to do may be quite different from that to which He calls you for He needs many kinds of co-workers.

Now the first kind of call that I find in the Bible is the way *God calls men out of a human situation.* Perhaps there is a very needy people. Maybe they need spiritual help, or maybe they need a message of love, or perhaps they need moral correction. But out of that situation of need, God sends His call. Do you remember the vision that came to Paul and the man from Macedonia? The words of the man from Macedonia were,

"Come over to Macedonia and help us," and God gave him a call through that situation of need in Macedonia (Acts 16:9). Do you remember the story of the Good Samaritan? He was a man who found a situation of need. The priest went by on one side and the Levite went by also, but God called the Samaritan to deal with the problem (Lk 10:33). Sometimes even today, there are needy situations in the world and God puts His finger on somebody and calls him, and says, "I want you to go there and deal with that problem."

Now, there are other times when the call of God comes in another way. When we think of *a work in which God wants somebody to help Him.* Think for a moment of the biblical words that God used to describe people who worked with Him. Sometimes they were referred to as His *servants* (Lk 16:13; Rom 16:1; I Cor 7:22; Phil 1:1; Col 4:12), and sometimes He spoke of his helpers as *harvesters* (Lk 10:2; Jn 4:35), and sometimes He said His stewards (Lk 16:1-12; I Cor 4:1-2; I Pet 4:10), and at other times He spoke of His *ambassadors* (2 Cor 5:20), and sometimes as His *co-workers* or *fellow workers* (2 Cor 6:1). Now, these are all the same kind of word because they imply *work.* They imply that it is God's work, and that God wants to make use of people to help him in His work. This kind of task means that those concerned must be *responsible.* He wants a good servant. Nobody wants a bad servant. If you have a household, or a vineyard, and you appoint a man as the steward over it, you want a man you can depend on. When a government or a King appoints an ambassador to another country he wants that ambassador to be a true spokesman for him. Thus, sometimes God calls us to help Him in His work, and to represent Him.

Now, there is still another way in which God calls people and that is *He calls men to proclaim His Word.* There are at least two ways in which He calls us to proclaim His Word. There is a time when we have to speak for social justice, as God called Amos to do when He sent him to Bethel to rebuke the people in that market centre for their dishonest trading (Amos 5:10-12). We meet a good deal of that in the Old Testament. But there is another way in which we can be sent to proclaim His Word, and that is to tell people of the Saviour and the way of salvation. Both of these are, in a way, prophetic ministries. They were prophetic because the man who was called was speaking for God. Before Amos spoke to the people at Bethel he said, "Thus saith the Lord," and this is where a *proclamation* is different from *dialogue,* and it is different also from *witness.*

The man who proclaims a thing is like a herald, an announcer, he is telling something that has been told to him for

publishing abroad. He received his instructions from a king
or a chief, or his boss. He received the word of someone
above him. But when God calls me to be a witness, He calls
me to tell what I know myself and what I have found to be true
about Him. You remember the man in the gospel story who was
cured of all the evil spirits, and Jesus said to him afterwards, "Now you go home to your people and tell what the Lord
has done for you" (Mk 5:19). Now he was called to witness,
because he was sharing his own experience of the Lord with his
friends at home. But when the preacher proclaims the Word
he is not just telling something he knows, he is telling a
word he has received from the Lord above.   So if I come to
talk with a Hindu and I want to discuss religion with him, I
get him to dialogue, so we may reason together. That is one
way. But proclamation is different from this. It is the word
of the king announced by his herald, and you cannot alter that.
You can't debate it. So sometimes God calls us to dialogue,
and sometimes He calls us to witness, and sometimes He calls
us to proclaim His Word. But it is God who calls and we must
obey.

When God calls someone he also *equips* him. (I Cor
12:4; Rom 12:6-8). God doesn't ask me to do something that I
couldn't possibly do. He gives me a gift. All the gifts I
have come from Him, and He says to me, "I want you to use these
gifts which I have given you for my work." And if he has
equipped me with gifts, and has called me to go and use those
gifts, then, I dare not say "No". When we are in work like
this we are *heirs of the promises* (Gal 3:29; Heb 6:17; 11:9),
and we are recipients of His gifts (I Cor 12-13). That makes
us doubly responsible for what we do.

In this way we are *involved in God's method*. God speaks
to men through men. So God has ordained it so that He is
ready and willing to depend on us to be faithful, and to do
His work. He gives us the Gospel so that we may give it to
others, and this is why Paul was able to speak of "*my* gospel
(Rom 2:16; 16:25). Of course it was "the Gospel of God," but
he could call it "my gospel," because it had been given to
him with the instructions that he should *transmit it to others*.

All these things are involved in the "call".   God
calls us. He gives us the gifts we need. He expects us to
use them and to do so to His glory. In this little book we
are concentrating particularly on one of those calls - the
call to go, and to proclaim the message of salvation. Sometimes the call comes to a church or a congregation, and the
congregation *sends* out one of its members as a missionary in
the Spirit (Acts 13:1-4). Sometimes the call comes direct to
an individual, and under the constraint of the Spirit the individual *goes*. They are the important words, the church *sends*

and the missionary *goes* (Mt 28:18-20). And that is the theological foundation on which I am putting together this book. Now we must ask some historical questions and answer them.

. . . .

Who sent the missionaries to evangelize the South Pacific? There were two great movements that swept across the Pacific in the last century. See the map (fig. 3). Now, when the Gospel first came to the Pacific, it was brought by the LMS missionaries from Britain. They settled in Tahiti; but the real diffusion of the Gospel across Polynesia started from the little island of Raiatea. It was really here where the movement began. The Gospel spread from that island in a westerly direction to a number of small island groups that were scattered over this vast ocean - Niue, Cook Islands and others. That was the first movement.

Another movement was begun in Sydney, Australia, and went to Tonga, and from Tonga it spread through the islands up to Samoa and across to Fiji. From Fiji it was spread to New Britain and New Ireland and also to Papua. Later it spread to the Solomon Islands and also to North Australia. The two movements met at Samoa, and they moved beyond Samoa to the New Hebrides. Now, the people of Polynesia has a similar language and so they could communicate without any trouble. But when they got over into Melanesia they had problems. Some of the sounds that they wanted to make in their words were very difficult for them to utter. They also moved up into the south of New Guinea.

The first movement can be traced back to the revival under Whitefield and the second had a connection with the revival under the Wesleys. So God used these movements away back in England to open the way for the work of evangelization in the South Pacific. However, most of the real evangelistic thrust in the Pacific was done by people from the islands of Fiji, Tonga and Samoa, and the little island of Raiatea, not by Europeans at all. As the years went by over three hundred native missionaries went out from Fiji alone into those islands to the northwest. But I want to tell you a little bit about these Pacific Island missionaries, from Tahiti to Fiji.

(1) There was a missionary named John Williams who was, in a way, a rebellious fellow. He did not always do what the Board Secretaries told him to do. They stationed him on the island of Raiatea. There were only four or five thousand people on the whole island, and there were four or five missionaries. Williams said, "Why should you confine me within a single reef when there are hundreds of islands in the Pacific

whose people have not heard the Gospel and we have four or
five missionaries on this small island?" Williams decided to
build himself a ship and sail outside the reefs of Raiatea.
He said, "If the Board won't shift me, then I'm going to shift
myself." But he could not have done that alone. He was able
to do it only because the people of Raiatea, like him, wanted
to be missionaries. He built his ship and took a group of
Raiatea missionaries on board with enough food for a long voyage (about 3,000 miles) and he plotted that voyage calling at
the Polynesian island groups on the way across the Pacific.
He planned to leave two of the Raiatea people at each island.
So who were the missionaries? The people of Raiatea were the
missionaries. Williams transported them, but *they* heard the
call of God to evangelize the other islands. John Williams
would go and speak to the King on one of these islands, and he
would preach the Gospel to him and say, "If I leave one of my
teachers with you to tell you more of the Gospel than I've
been able to tell you, will you receive him? Can he have a
house and a garden? Will you protect him until I come back
again?" And if the King said "Yes" he left Raiatea missionaries on the island. Then he sailed away and came to Tonga.
From Tonga he went to Samoa, as I described in the last chapter.

Now, when Williams came back a few months later to these
small islands, in many cases he found a church there. So who
planted the church in all those islands? Not the white missionary, but the people of Raiatea. How did John Williams prepare these people when he took them on to the boat and sailed
off into the west? He called them all together and spoke to
them about the Christian mission, and he told them four things
he wanted them to remember. These were the four principles of
John Williams' missionary message. He said - "First, you are
chosen by your church at Raiatea, they send you." This was
just like what happened at Antioch (Acts 13:1-4). In the second place he said, "You are going to the land where God leads
you." Remember the phrase in the Old Testament, "the place the
Lord shall choose" (Dt 14:25; 16:6,11,16; 18:6, &c.). So you
see they went in faith knowing that God would open up the way
for them somewhere. The third thing he told them was based on
the Great Commission. He said, "When you go to the far distant
islands, remember the Lord promised that he would be with you
'even unto the end'" (Mt 28:20). There had been a great spiritual movement in Raiatea and the guidance of the Holy Spirit
had been sought for the venture. The fourth thing that Wil-
iams gave to these people was a promise - "What God has done
for you in Raiatea He will do also for the people in the places
where you go with His Gospel." They went out in front of the
white missionaries. They planted churches and God really
blessed their work.

(2) Now very briefly, let me tell you about the movement from Tonga. There had been missionaries in Tonga away
back, more than thirty years before, but the place was hard
and there was no response. It was just like a field that was
not ready for harvest. But now at this time when the Gospel
arrived the field was 'ripe unto harvest'. An experience
called the Great Awakening swept through Tonga and in three
years the whole country had become Christian. The Tongans
were great sailors. They had big canoes and they used to
sail to and from Samoa and Fiji. There were big Fiji canoes
also, and all along the windward side of Fiji there were people who could speak the Tongan language. So these people had
relationships with each other and used to trade with each
other. The Tongans were good dealers. They were good carpenters and good carvers. They used to go to Fiji to get the
wood for making their canoes and other artifacts. Soon after
the Great Tongan Awakening the Gospel spread all along these
trade routes. These are what are sometimes spoken of as
"Bridges of God" - i.e., the bridges along which the message
went from one people to another.

Shortly I shall be telling you the story of a Tongan
called Joeli Bulu. He was converted in Tonga, and when he
had been a Christian for only about a year he went to Fiji as
a missionary and lived there for forty years planting
the church in all parts of that country. At that time Fiji
was a wild country where the people were cannibals. One of
the most wonderful stories I know tells how this cannibal people became Christian. Fiji is the biggest of all these island groups, and the biggest island, Viti Levu, is about 4,500
square miles. It has a mountainous centre with many rivers
and the Gospel began to grow wherever the Tongan settlements
were situated. The first converts in Fiji were Tongans, but
they began to win the Fijians as the Gospel spread out from
the Christian settlements along the coast. After about 25
years all the coastal people had been won to the Lord, and
then the Gospel began to spread inland following the river
courses until it reached the mountain tribes in the interior.
These were quite a different people from those down along the
coast and they spoke a different language. So it took maybe
nearly 50 years before all Fiji was won for Christ, but all
the pioneering work done both along the coast and in the interior was mainly accomplished by Fijian converts. The Christian people of Fiji saw the interior of their land as their
own mission field. These tribes lived in fortresses in the
mountains and many exciting stories could be told of how the
coastal Christian catechists went up into the mountains and
risked their lives to give the Gospel to the people of the interior.

Now the time came when all the interior was won for
Christ and the young Fijian Church asked itself the questions,
"When all of our people have turned from their old religion
is our missionary work finished?" "What do we do then?" Then
they answered their own questions - "We must go to other islands, because there are still many other islands which have
never heard the Gospel." It was that kind of thinking that
led to Fijian missionary expansion into the islands in the west.
And I want to tell you what I think is one of the most wonderful stories in the planting of the church in the South Pacific.

(3) Fiji became a British Colony in 1874, (the church
was in Fiji long before the country became a Colony) and this
was about the same time as the Fijians were beginning to ask
if they should have a mission field outside their own islands.
They decided on an agreement with the Church in Australia.
The Australian Church would supply the ships and all the material and money that was needed for a new mission. But Fiji
would supply the missionaries. They would be island missionaries. This was agreed, but just about the time they were
ready to go, Fiji was hit by a measles epidemic. This terrible
epidemic swept right through the islands and 40,000 Fijians
died of the disease. In some places there were many pastors
and teachers who died. I know of one part of Fiji that lost
200 Christian pastor-teachers. In this great trouble the
question came up, "What about our mission? We have no pastors
for our own churches, or pastor-teachers for the smaller
churches, how can we send people to a foreign land if we can't
look after our own church at home?" There were some who were
talking that way. Then a ship came in from Australia bringing
Dr. Brown, the Head of the Mission Board from that country.
This was the first ship to come to Fiji after the measles epidemic, and Dr. Brown looked at the state of things in Fiji
and saw how they had been devastated by this disease. "I have
hardly the heart to ask these people to give up some of their
very few teachers and pastors who are left," he said, "but I
will go to the theological institution and tell them what my
purposes were in case there are perchance some who will go
with me." So he spoke to the students in the theological
institution and said,"You know how we had planned to have a
mission to New Guinea. We had planned to take teachers and
pastors from this country, but you have suffered from the
measles epidemic and lost so many people that I really don't
know what to do. I am wondering if there is perhaps someone
among you students who would volunteer to go with me to New
Guinea?" Then the Principal of the school said,"Well, don't
ask them to make their decision now. Let them think it over
and pray about it for tonight and tomorrow we will talk about
it." So the students talked it over with their wives that

night, and they prayed. Then on the following day the 84
theological students gathered together and sat down quietly.
The Principal of the school stood up and said, "Now I would
like to know if anyone among you is willing to go to New Guinea
with Dr. Brown. If so, will he please stand up." What do you
think happened? Every one of the 84 stood up! Well, Dr.
Brown's problems were solved to a certain degree, but now he
had other problems because he didn't need 84 missionaries!
Neither could the home church in Fiji spare them. The required
number had to be selected.

And then they began to get travelling papers and visas
ready; and some outside gossip circulated a story they they
"were being compelled to go." So the Administrator of the
country called them all together, and he said to them,"I want
you to know that nobody can *make* you go. You don't have to go
unless you *want* to go." But God had spoken to these men and
they did want to go. Then the Administrator began talking
more strongly to them, trying to discourage them. He said,
"Do you people want to die in a foreign land?" (And you know
that is a hard word for a Fijian, because when a Fijian is
dying he wants to go to his own land.) Dr. Brown tells in his
diary that when that question was asked he feared greatly, but
after this discouragement had gone on for some time, the Fijian leader of the group, whose name was Aminio Baledrokadroka,
stood up. He thought that these obstructions of the Administrator had gone far enough, and this is what he said to the
Administrator in the presence of everybody, "We have fully considered this matter and our minds are made up. No one has
pressed us in any way. We have heard the call of God, we have
given ourselves to God's work, and it is our mind to go to
New Guinea. If we live, we live. If we die, we die." That
was the end of the matter. And they went. And most of them
died. But they planted the church, and that church is still
there and very much alive. It is a missionary church itself
to this day, and even World War II could not wipe it out.

Fig. 3

The Messenger of Peace (See page 8)

3

Missionary Penetration

We now turn to the subject of *missionary penetration,*
and in order to understand this clearly we will first make use
of a biblical model. Look at the 16th chapter of Acts. It is
a fairly long passage, but read it as a whole account of one
of Paul's missionary journeys. He has been to Derbe and Lys-
tra and to Iconium. You could take a map and follow him
through verses 6, 7 and 8 until he reached Troas, where he related an experience he had (v.9-10). Then the journey went on
by boat until he reached Philippi in Macedonia (v.12). His experiences there continue until the end of the chapter. This
is a very important chapter in the missionary story. One of
the first things that we see is that Paul had his own plan to
go into Northern Galatia, into Bithynia, and the Lord stopped
him. And so the Lord turned Paul away from Bithynia into the
direction of Troas. Here is the missionary problem of *the two
wills* - my will and the Lord's will. Paul's own idea and God's
idea, and because Paul responded to God's idea and went to
Troas he got God's message when he reached there. He didn't
get his call in Galatia, he got his call at Troas. Sometimes
we have our own ideas and the Lord changes them, then it seems
very mysterious to us because we had thought the plan out so
well. But when we really do what God wants us to do then all
of a sudden the true meaning of everything comes to us.   So
Paul went to Troas, and there he had the vision of the man
from Macedonia, and then obediently he went over into Macedonia.

In the two studies we have had, we discussed first the
will of God and then the power of God.   In this study we
are going to see what happened when Paul was obedient to the
Lord by responding to the vision and going to Macedonia. He
still had to penetrate the Macedonian situation. He   knew

God was with him, but now he was looking at the mission field
- the first mission field in Europe. Notice that the Gospel
went from Asia into Europe, not from Europe into Asia.   The
leading that Paul got from the Lord took him to the main city
of Macedonia. This was Philippi. Philippi was a Roman colony.
It wasn't an old Greek city with a long history like Athens,
it was a new and modern city built by the Romans to quarter a
garrison of soldiers there, to keep the peace in that part of
the world. All kinds of people had gathered there. It had a
mixed population - quite interracial.

The interracial character of this city is seen in the
stories that are told in this chapter, because each story
comes from a different racial setting. There is a story about
a Jewish proselyte, a woman who is a craft worker, who makes
purple cloth, and sells it. She was a migrant, having come
from Thyatira, in Asia Minor. And then there is the story of
the Greek slave girl who was possessed by a demon. She was a
Greek. She was a European, of the first part of Europe that
Paul came to. Then there was the Roman jailer who had come
from Rome, in Italy, away over in the west. So here is the
situation that Paul is meeting as a missionary. You know
Paul himself was a native of Tarsus, away in the east. Paul
had been travelling through southern Galatia with a plan to
go north into Bithynia, on the Black Sea, but God had turned
him aside and sent him to Troas. Paul planned to preach to
people who belonged to Asia Minor as he himself did. However,
God was saying "I want you as a missionary for the Gentiles.
I want you to go to the nations where Asians, Greeks and Ital-
ians live in a mixed racial position." God was making Paul
realize that he couldn't go just where he himself wanted to
go, he had to go where God wanted to use him. That is the
situation we have in this chapter. Paul is going to plant a
church in this city. We know he did that very thing and left
a house church there (v.40).

There are a number of interesting stories in this chapter. One very interesting point, for instance, is that here
there is a *small group conversion* - the conversion and baptism
of a whole family unit. The whole household became Christian
at one time. Another missionary idea that we get in this
chapter is the idea of *the house church*. Remember when Paul
was leaving the city - "And they went out of the prison and
entered into the house of Lydia: and when they had seen the
brethren they comforted them, and departed" (v.40). They had
already got together a fellowship of people there. Another
thing that is found in this chapter is that Paul came face to
face with a person possessed by a demon. In one of the Gospel
accounts of the Great Commission the apostles were told to
cast out demons (Mk 16:17). In one of the chapters that is to

come later I am going to talk about this kind of power encounter.

Another interesting thing about this account is that
when Paul came to this city he knew where to go. How? Now,
if he had lived in our day he probably would have had a letter of introduction to someone. But Paul knew that there were
bound to be some people who worshipped the God of Israel (pro-
selytes) somewhere in the city. This kind of person existed
in most of the big cities of the Roman Empire, and Paul knew
that they quite often met outside, often beside the river. So
Paul followed his knowledge of the custom of these people,
and sure enough, at the riverside on the Sabbath, they were
there worshipping. Paul often used the proselyte as a bridge
for gospel preaching. He knew that the proselyte believed in
the God of Israel and could start his message from that point.
Paul was quite a good anthropologist, he knew that a good way
to communicate was to start with something the people knew,
something of their own, and then to move on to the new thing
about the Gospel. He could quote their poetry and their prov-
erbs, and he knew when to be like a Roman and when to be like
a Greek and when to be like a Jew, and he used these contacts
for the effective preaching of the Gospel.

Now I really must get to the South Pacific, and that's
a long way from Greece! All these principles that we find in
this chapter that tell how Paul was able to penetrate a new
situation are found in mission fields all over the world.
Paul now found himself in a new situation. He had an interracial group of people meeting at Philippi and the church
there became one of the great New Testament churches. The important word here is *situation - missionary situation* - so I
want to ask the question, "What kind of a situation was there
in the South Pacific when the first missionaries arrived?"
I can only describe this very briefly. When the first missionaries came to the South Pacific many of the islands were in a
state of war. Sometimes one island was at war with another
island, and sometimes a kingdom with a kingdom. There were
about 280 islands in the Fiji group and they were divided into seven kingdoms. One of these kingdoms was fighting against
another, and at the same time little tribal groups within the
kingdom were fighting with each other. The Fijian people,
and some of the other island groups were, then, a warlike people. Many of their customs were built around the idea of war.
I think I could give you the names of about 20 or 25 different Fijian war clubs. They had a group of clubs that were
smashers, for smashing down on the head, breaking the skull.
They also had a group of clubs that were thrust into you and
pierced you. Another group of clubs was designed to cut off
your head, and they had still another club that had a head

like a pineapple with a little knob on the end of it.   The
man who used this club used to hit his enemy's head then pull
the club back with a flick of the wrist so that it didn't
smash the head but left a clean hole in the skull.   And then
there was the throwing club.   A warrior had two clubs – one in
his belt and one over his shoulder.   When his enemy came along
the path he would try to get him with the throwing club, and
if he missed then he would club him with the other one. These
were the customs that were practised before the Gospel came
to Fiji.   Then with the war there was also the practice of
cannibalism.   They had many ways of killing a man and cooking
him.   This cannibalism was ceremonial and it was part of their
religion.   Then they practised what we call patricide (killing your father).   If a man was thought to be too old and
couldn't do his work properly, his son would kill him.   Probably the old man had done this to his father when he was young.
The young man would come to his father and say, "Sir, your
sun has set," and he would club him.   I'm merely trying to
show you what the *situation* was when the first missionaries
arrived.   It is important that you see the situation. This is
what the missionaries had to face.   The people also practised
widow-strangling.   This was a religious belief too, because
these people believed in a life to come, and if a chief or a
warrior or a priest – somebody with status – died, and he
knew that when he died he would go to the afterworld, he wanted to take his wives with him.   Now, this was not only to
serve the spirit of the man after he died, but also to give
him status so that everyone in the afterworld would know he
was a big chief.   In his life on earth he had many wives and
he had many servants, and sometimes the servants and some
warriors too would go with him by being buried in his grave.
There was a good reason for this belief.   If a man was a very
great warrior, or a very great chief, or a magic man, he would
become a god after he died; and if all these customs were not
performed, then, as a god, he would be angry and he would not
give the people good magic or victory in war.

      In some countries in the Pacific, instead of cannibal-
ism they practised head-hunting. This too was a religious idea,
if you could get the head of your enemy you could control his
power. In the Solomon Islands they had small houses with trays
on which they kept a row of the skulls of their enemies.   The
more skulls you had the more power you had. They used to per-
form religious rites at these trays to get the power, then
make use of it in war and in magic.

      Very soon after the first western navigators discovered
the Pacific, they were followed by white adventurers, whalers
and sandalwood traders.   They were there to make a profit out
of the islands, and introduced western firearms and ammunition.

Some island peoples were warlike before this; and fought with spears, clubs, and bows and arrows. But once they had western arms and ammunition war became a terrible thing, especially when a white sandalwooder became involved in a war between two island chiefs. This was the state of affairs when the first missionaries arrived.

What is more, the white sailors introduced liquor, and that also did a great deal of harm in the islands. Not only did they teach the islanders to drink liquor, they taught them how to make it. There is probably no greater cause than liquor that has decreased the population of true Hawaiians in Hawaii, for example. So war and cannibalism and everything else got completely out of control, and about the time the missionaries came many people were already tired of the wars. Many said, "We are ready to give up our gods and our old ways." So there were two kinds of islands that the first missionaries found. There were those islands where the people still practised and believed in the old customs, and there were those islands where the people were tired of the old ways and wanted to get rid of them. So you have the islands where the people did not want the Gospel, and you have the islands where the people were ready to listen to the Gospel. This is what, in church growth studies, we call a "ripe field" and an "unripe field."

Let me give you an example of a small island where the people were tired of war and where they had had an epidemic in which many of them died. They were saying, "Our gods can't even look after us." There was a man called Wai who was a herald. He felt this as a burden on his heart, "My people are suffering from war and disease and our gods can't look after us. Can I not find a way to solve this problem?" On a business trip to Lakeba, he met another Fijian called Takai. Takai was a lesser chief, but he had travelled far on the white men's ships. He had been to Tahiti, and he had been as far as Sydney, Australia. He had also been to Tonga, and the ship on which he sailed had visited Tonga at the time of the Great Awakening - the original people movement from heathenism to Christianity. And Takai said, "This is a good thing, this is a way to end the wars, I would like an evangelist or a teacher to go with me to my island." Later on he succeeded in getting an evangelist, but at the time of this story he had not done so. When Wai met Takai he told him about the damage of the wars and disease that had come to Fiji, and about the liquor that was on his island, and how he desired to have the new way of life. And Takai told Wai about the movement of Christianity he had seen in Tonga, and Wai went back to his island with a great desire to have Christianity there. He knew nothing about the Christian way of life. He was not a Christian. He had never met Christ himself, he had only heard about what Christianity had done for Tonga. All he knew of Christianity

was that Christians kept the seventh day holy. So he went
back to his island and he talked to all the people about this
new thing called Christianity. They talked it over in the
village council and were all of one mind, they had had enough
of war, and they had had enough of sickness, and they wanted
a God who could look after them. They wanted to be Christian.
But how could they become Christian without a preacher? So
Wai said, "Let us worship God on every seventh day." On every seventh day everyone dressed up in his gala clothes. They
did no work on that day. They came together to worship. But,
nobody knew how to worship, so Wai went along to the pagan
chief and to the pagan priest. This was the priest who worshipped the local gods: the heathen gods. And Wai dragged
him along to their worship service and said to him. "We want
to worship Jehovah. Now you pray to Him for us." He stood
over the pagan priest until he began to pray. And he prayed
like this -

Oh, Lord Jehovah, these people want to worship You.
I'm not speaking for myself. I want to serve other
gods. But please look after them and bless them. Amen.

Look at all the forces that are at work here. Look at
the field ready for harvest. If only there had been a missionary there to help, or an evangelist. Let me ask a question,
"Do you think God answered that strange prayer?" Certainly
he answered it. About that time there was a canoe sailing out
at sea and somehow it was turned off its course in a storm.
It came to shelter at a very small island about fifty miles
away from this one. Now, nearly all the people on that canoe
were heathens, but there were a few Christians. They were
Tongans, because the Gospel had not yet been heard by the Fijians. There was a young Christian on the canoe who had prayed
with the other Christians in the storm for God to save them.
And when the wind blew them to this island they heard about
what was going on in Ono (the other small island where Wai
lived). The young Christian's name was Josaia. On that small
island God called Josaia and said to him, "I want you to go to
Ono, the island where Wai lives." And Josaia went to the island, just as Ananaias was sent to Paul, and he told the people of the Gospel. This was before there were any missionaries in the islands of Fiji. God himself was surely working
there beforehand.

At the same time, in Tonga, the Tongan converts were
praying about Fiji and they were getting together a party to
go to Fiji. When the first missionary actually reached the
island where Wai was, more than a year later, he found a little Christian church there, both a congregation and a building,
and they had actually sent some of their number to tell the
Gospel to their relatives on other islands. The missionary

found 328 adult Christians waiting for baptism. Now, did God answer that pagan priest's prayer?

There is a New Testament ring about this account of *penetrating the situation* in Ono. The Book of Acts is an account of missionary penetration. Every new missionary in the South Pacific who went to another island had his own kind of situation to penetrate. Now I want to raise the question of the strategy that was used by the missionaries when they penetrated such an island situation. We always need some kind of strategy in order to get into the situation.

If I may generalize for the South Pacific at large I suppose there were three or four things that were very important. First, when the missionaries learned the customs of the people and respected them - i.e., the customs of procedure, not customs like cannibalism - and when they learned to operate through the regular social procedures and through the proper leaders and spokesmen, they usually had good responses to their message if the time was ripe.

Second, when the missionaries learned the language of the people and reduced it to writing, translating the Scriptures and preparing catechisms, hymn books and other aids to worship, again they had good responses. The people of the South Pacific soon became people of the Book.

Third, the planting of the church in the Pacific usually followed one of two patterns. I would call one a pattern of *programmed action* and I would call the second a pattern of *pentecostal experience*. Furthermore, the Lord frequently opened great opportunities for witness in heathen situations. Let me give you one or two examples of these principles.

I said that the missionaries used the customary procedures for approaching people. In most of these societies they had a *herald*. The herald is the man who comes between the person with the message and the person who hears the message. Even to this day I would not go into a Fijian village without a companion - that man would be my herald. From olden times in Fijian life there has been a herald between the chief and the people, and the will of the chief was passed down to the people through the herald. And the views of the people were carried back to the chief by the herald. He was a very important man in Fijian society. Sometimes, in the olden days, they used to call the herald "the stomach of evil," because if the chief and the people didn't get on very well together the herald would declare the chief's words in a nice way to the people, and he would transmit the people's reply in a nice way to the chief. He "swallowed the evil" as it were, and thus he helped the society to operate smoothly. So the herald was an important man who held the society together, and every time a missionary went to a Fijian village he should have been accompanied by a herald, because that was *the right way to do it*. Even if the people did not accept the Gospel message, at least they would listen to him, if he went with a herald. The early missionaries in the Pacific all used heralds.

There was a herald whose name was Mateinaniu. He was also a dancing master and he had trained a lot of men in a very fine war dance. This was before the Gospel came to Fiji, and at that time there was a high chief from Tonga visiting Lau, who said, "I would like to take Mateinaniu with me to Tonga to teach this war dance to my people." So Mateineniu sailed away to Tonga with the high chief. It happened that he arrived in Tonga at the time of the Great Awakening. (An Awakening is like a Revival. The difference being that an Awakening comes to people who have never been Christian before, and a Revival happens where the people are nominal Christians being revived.)

Now the chief, who thought the people would like to learn the war dance, found that they had turned against pagan war and were looking to the Lord. What is more, Mateinaniu got involved in the Awakening and became converted. In Tonga he talked about his own country which was still in a state of cannibalism, and he said, "This Awakening is a great thing, my people ought to hear about it." The Tongan converts were saying, "Yes, there are all those cannibals over in Fiji; we ought to take the Gospel over to them." Then, in response to the leading of the Spirit of God, two missionaries and a party of Tongan missionaries prepared to go to Fiji.

The missionaries said, "If we are going to give the Gospel to Fiji we will have to know the Fijian language." So Mateinaniu who had now taken a Christian name, Josua, taught the missionaries some Fijian. Instead of teaching the war dance, he became a translator of the Gospel. And as the time grew near he became very excited about going back to Fiji with the missionary party. But Mateinaniu knew that no one would ever listen to the Gospel, no chief would ever let a man hear the Gospel unless he heard it through a herald. So Mateinaniu became the herald of the first missionary party. He knew how to do it. He knew how to open the door. He knew the right kind of ceremonial language to use, because the chiefly people of Lau have a language they use when they speak to workmen, and another quite different language when they speak to a high chief. There are two ways of talking to a man, one is polite, and one is not polite. So Mateinaniu was able to take the first missionary party right into the presence of the Paramount Chief at Lakeba, and introduce the Gospel in the polite and correct way. And because of that, the Chief replied, "The visitors may live here, we'll give them a house

and we'll let them talk to us over the next few days." Now,
if they had not gone in the right way they would have been
enemies. They might even have been put in the cannibal oven!
So you see the Lord provided a herald to bring the Gospel to
Fiji and to gain a hearing in the Group. There are many stories like this about the importance of customary procedure that
could be told.

Now let us look at the matter of *programmed action*.
Let me tell you of three ways in which the Gospel was spread
by a program in the South Pacific. The first is the story of
a man called Wilisoni Lagi. Wilisoni was the first Fijian
minister to be trained also as a doctor. He lived a little
later then Mateinaniu, in the time when they had medical training in Fiji, and the country had accepted Christianity. Lagi
took the Gospel to Papua, in South New Guinea, and he worked
with an Australian doctor. Remember, Wilisoni was both a
minister and a doctor, and this is probably the only medical
missionary story that I will have to tell you.

In Papua they began by building a hospital, and they
said, "We want the sick people from around this area to come
into the hospital. However, we don't want to bring in all the
people who have minor injuries like a cut finger or a stomach
ache or headache, or something like that, because there are
many more serious diseases than there are facilities in the
hospital." So they agreed to work together as a team. They
worked out an itineration system through the villages. Lagi
would go around the villages one week and the Australian doctor would be at the hospital, and the next week they would
exchange roles. The man on the village rounds would deal with
all the minor illnesses and would send the serious cases to
the hospital. Both in the village and at the hospital they
witnessed to the people about Jesus. Now, remember this was
a pioneering mission. There had never been a church there
before. However, after five or six years of this kind of
ministry there was a ring of Christian villages right around
the hospital where the people had accepted the Gospel. That
successful work was the result of a planned program.

A very different kind of program was used by a Church
of England missionary called Bishop Patteson. Patteson was
actually, in the end, killed by the people of one of the islands. But during his ministry he served the Lord well. His
headquarters were on Norfolk Island and he itinerated in a
boat from island to island all through the South Pacific Ocean
asking the chiefs on the islands to which he went, "Do you
have any young men who will come with me and study in my
school?" And they would go with him for three or four months
in the season of the year that was not busy, and then he would

take them back to their islands for the busy season.   Then
again the next year he would take them back to his station
for some gospel lessons.   In this way they learned much about
the Bible and Christianity. When they returned to their home
islands they talked about what they had learned.   In this way
many churches sprang up in the islands where Bishop Patteson's
students came from.   The method had some dangers.   It was always possible for young men who went to a school like this to
become western and to be misfits when they returned to their
own islands. But Patteson was very careful of this, he knew
hundreds of islands and he spoke 30 different languages, and
so he tried to see that their training suited their life in
the place where they were going.   In a later chapter I will
tell you about one of these young men who became a very effective church planter after his training.   That was a second
kind of planned action, a strategy to penetrate a situation.

A third kind of planned action is a movement known as
the Melanesian Brotherhood.   This is a body of men who have
bound themselves together to be evangelists in other islands.
It is something like an old monastic order of Europe, except
that it was very mobile, and it was a Melanesian idea.   The
man who had this idea was a Solomon Islander called Ini Kopura.
He had read some European church history and he asked, "Why
can't we have a Melanesian movement like this?" He appealed
to the Bishop.   The Bishop approved and it was established.
The Melanesian Brotherhood still works today. When I was in
the Solomon Islands I met a number of the brothers.   They wore
a uniform comprising a black shirt and a black *sulu*, or *lap-
lap*.   But more important they have a planned program - a strategy for evangelism.   They try to find out where there is a
part of some island that has never heard the Gospel, and then
they say, "Two of our brothers will go to be evangelists to
that island or region."   Some of them are at present in New
Guinea, and others are in their own islands in the mountains
where the hill tribes have still not yet all become Christian.
They live in the village and build themselves a house like the
people use.   They learn the language and stay there until the
people want to become Christian as a group, or village. Then
they send a message to their Order and say, "These people are
ready to be made into a congregation."   A native pastor then
goes to the mountain village or to the island concerned, to
take the place of the brothers who now move to a new mission
field, leaving a church and pastor behind them.   So they go
from place to place bringing people to Christ, and leaving only
when the converts have been formed into churches.

Now God has blessed many of these programmed actions
and many of them have brought about very fine churches.   But
there are also other times when people have had a *pentecostal*

experience, when nothing had been planned at all. The people had just been at prayer or at worship. These pentecostal movements often happened during baptismal services. I have read about several in the journals of the early missionaries. One, I remember, from the journal of John Hunt, who tells of how he was in a baptismal service and there were about 10 candidates for baptism. At the moment he was about to baptize them, the highest lady of the land (you might call her the Queen of the island), suddenly burst into tears and could not control herself. Then someone else nearby also began to cry, and someone else over there. The Queen fainted, and they revived her. She fainted again, and when she was revived the second time she said to the pastor, "I know that I'm a sinner and I must get right with God. Can I make use of your little room there beside the church?" So she went there and struggled with God until she found peace. This sort of thing happened in place after place, in Fiji, from about the 10th to the 20th year of the mission. So I must say that though the church grew in many ways by strategic planning (for the Spirit of God did bless these systematic evangelists), there were other times when it just grew because God poured His Spirit out on the people, and some of these were marvellous experiences. Experiences of great power which cannot be explained in any other way than that God was at work.

I have seen the record of a worship service which was being held in the island of Kadavu where I lived for three years with my wife and children. We were the only white people on the whole island. I know the place where this happened away back in the early days when a worship service was being held. This was at the time the Gospel was just beginning to spread in that island. Among the converts who were in the worship service were a number of young women who, shortly before their conversion had been betrothed to a number of cannibal young men. These young men were afraid that if the girls remained Christian they would not be able to marry them. This made them very angry, not with the missionaries, but with the girls for becoming Christian, and they decided to break up the church service. They armed themselves with war clubs and marched around the church shouting their war cry. They cried out, "We are going to come in and club all you Christians!" They rushed in through the door. The first man bounded into the church with his club held high, then suddenly fell to the floor and couldn't get up. The second man came in after him, and he too fell to the floor. And then the third, until the whole lot of them were there on the floor like a heap of paralyzed bodies. In spite of this disturbance the service was not broken up. Afterwards these young men said they could not help themselves, that some great force had come over them and had

overpowered them. And the name of the Lord was praised mightly
in that place as the Gospel spread from village to village
through the whole island of Kadavu.

So God has built His Church in various ways. Sometimes
he has used the planned programs and strategy of His faithful
servants, and at other times He has suddenly poured out His
Spirit on people at prayer and worship. The Christian missionary thrust penetrating the island situation is a wonderful
story which should not be allowed to be forgotten. If God has
done it before, using humble people, is there any reason why
He cannot do it again?

4
Missionary Trials

The narrative of South Sea Island missions certainly has many accounts of glorious victory, but no reader can be anything but sobered by the grim episodes of suffering and persecution that accompany them. If we turn again to the Apostle Paul we discover that this had also been his experience of trial -

> ... in stripes above measure, in prisons more frequent, in deaths oft. Of the Jews five times received I forty stripes save one. Thrice was I beaten with rods, once was I stoned, thrice I suffered shipwreck, a night and a day I have been in the deep; in journeyings often, in perils of waters, in perils of robbers, in perils by mine own countrymen, in perils by the heathen, in perils in the city, in perils in the wilderness, in perils in the sea, in perils among false brethern; in weariness and painfulness, in watchings often, in hunger and thirst, in fastings often, in cold and nakedness (II Cor 11:23-27).

In the face of that kind of a record of suffering endured by the great missionary pioneer it certainly wouldn't be fair to point out all the missionary triumphs of the South Pacific without indicating something of the physical cost that went with them. Missionary work is not easy. Christians were never promised freedom from physical strain as they set out to evangelize and witness in the pagan world.

There are many reasons why the pioneer missionary may have to suffer. It may be because of persecution when the new Way seems to threaten the old way or the pagan religious system. Such persecution may come from one's own family, as Joeli Bulu experienced in Tonga when he wanted to become

Christian against his family cohesion in heathenism. Or it
may come from the priests and sorcerers when they feel their
positions, authority or wealth are threatened by the new
religion. It may be petty persecution, like stealing the
food supplies and destroying gardens; or it may be murder.
Many early Fijian Christians were killed and eaten in cannibal times. Many of the early island evangelists suffered
from sickness. Especially does one suffer if he is sick in
a foreign land where there are no doctors and he is far from
home. Or he may suffer because he works for years and years
and no one listens to him and he get no response – he may
suffer because he feels he has failed. Or he may suffer because of his own mistakes. I am not going to deal with the
mistakes that cause our suffering. Usually we know why we
made a mistake and we know why we suffer, but I want to talk
about these other kinds of sufferings – these three kinds.

In the last chapter I told you about Aminio Baledrokadroka, the man who spoke when the Fijians went to New Guinea,
you remember, "If we live we live, if we die we die." Yes,
these Fijians were going to the islands of New Britain and
New Ireland, just to the north of New Guinea. When the party
arrived, Aminio, the leader, who remembered how the Gospel
had come to Fiji and been received by his own people, called
them all together. He was sending them out into the villages
diffusing his forces among people who had heard nothing of
the Gospel. He warned them –

> For some time you will find that things will be alright.
> But when you begin to be effective as evangelists: when
> you begin to win converts to the Lord, then your day of
> persecution will begin. There will be people who will
> set their hearts against you, and against your Gospel.
> There are people who make great profit out of their re-
> ligion – the priests – they will be against you. The
> first little time will be easy, but when you run into
> persecution, then you will have to prove yourselves good
> soldiers by enduring hardness.

Now, he was older than the rest of the party. He was
a senior man, and he was old enough to remember that this was
what happened in Fiji. Surely it would happen again. Satan
does not like losing his followers. This pioneering party
really suffered. About a third of them died of sickness and
never saw their homeland again, and all of them were persecuted because they won converts.

Now the classical passage in the Bible for the missionary or evangelist enduring suffering is found in the same
Pauline letter – II Cor 4:8 – 5:1. There are five very important points it makes about the Christian suffering in his

evangelistic work. First, suffering may mean trouble or
death to us, but it may mean life to someone else. Second,
Christ is our model, he shows us how to suffer and how to
endure suffering. Third, the ultimate end of our suffering
is, somehow, that God should be glorified. We don't live for
ourselves, we live for God. Fourth, even if our physical
body suffers the inner man is strengthened and enriched; and
fifth, in any case, the physical body is a temporary thing -
we remember the resurrection of Christ and our expectations
in the life to come. If we endure our hardness in these
sufferings, in these ways it will work out in the end to the
glory of God - that is what Paul is saying.

However, there is a question that arises, namely,
"How does God use a situation of suffering, to work out His
glory?" I believe that our vision is narrow and confined.
If I look at the moments of my life when I've been troubled
and in suffering, from a distance, the suffering seems very
small. The burdens were very heavy at the time, but as I
look back now the suffering was "but for a moment" in the
whole of my lifetime. And as I look back over history - the
years of suffering - I find it very difficult to remember a
single time of suffering that God wasn't working some way or
other to bless me. Jesus spoke in terms of a cross for those
who follow him, and when he sent out those preachers in the
days of his flesh, he said, "I am sending you as lambs among
wolves." A man needs courage and fortitude to be an evangelist of the Lord. He never promised an easy road, but he did
promise that his presence would be with us "even unto the
end," and he was implying that when we are suffering in his
name he is with us.

Now I want to look at a few cases of how the missionaries of the Pacific - the island missionaries as well as the
western missionaries - suffered to the glory of God.

In the year 1867, an English missionary named Thomas
Baker took a party of Fijian evangelists, one ordained minister, and a number of evangelist teachers, into the highlands
of Viti Levu, the biggest of the Fiji islands. The centre
of this island is a great plateau which is drained by several
major river systems. The headwaters of the Rewa - the Wai-
dina, Wainibuka and Wainimala flow east and southeast from a
high mountain ridge, the Sigatoka flows to the Southwest and
the Ba River to the west. This episode took place in the
mountain villages of that dividing range. Thomas Baker was
appointed to a place a few miles up the Rewa River, in 1866,
and designated "missionary to the interior." The mountain
people differed from those on the coast. The former were
still pagan, the latter Christian. They spoke different

languages. The mountaineers differed greatly in physique and they were quite savage. At about this time there were many conversions through this river basin. The Gospel was spreading along the Rewa River and up its tributaries. This part of Fiji was certainly "ripe unto harvest." On the way into the interior the Christian party had some hundreds of baptisms.

Baker planned to follow this river, to cross the dividing range and go down one of the western rivers to the coast. But when they passed over the range they found that the people along the western rivers did not want the Gospel. The party was attacked by cannibals who were concealed in the bushes beside the mountain track on which they were travelling. Suddenly, at a given cry, the cannibals fell on the Christian party and, except for two who escaped into the bush, all were killed, cooked and eaten - Thomas Baker, Setareki Seileka and the Christian evangelists. It shows the great price which any missionary may be asked to pay at any time. When James Calvert was asked by someone who had heard a lot of stories like this, "Weren't you afraid to be with people like this? Weren't you afraid to die?" Calvert replied, "No, we died before we went." They had given their lives to Christ for him to use in any way. Hundreds of Christian evangelists made this same decision in Fiji alone - and I could tell you the names of a score or more who died this way in the faith.

Now this story is a good illustration of how even environment can effect evangelism. There were no roads in the interior of Fiji and the lines of communication were the river systems. There had been more culture contact in the eastern river systems, and the villages along the Rewa and its tributaries were, in biblical terms, "a field ripe unto harvest". The mission station was down near the coast just above the river delta, and commanded the waterways going inland. It was a good strategic position. But over the mountains on the western side there had been no culture contact to speak of, no mission station and no gospel penetration. The field was certainly not ready for harvest. Between the eastern and western river systems was a mountain wall. If Thomas Baker had realized that he may not have tried to go that way. The better way may have been to start at the western river mouth and to have worked up into the interior over a period of time.

That was 1867. In 1874, only seven years later, a large party of Fijians went to New Britain, and within 10 years of the founding of that mission they had paid any 1867 debt Fiji had to Christain mission. They paid it in kind and they paid it in full. The party, led by Sailasa Naucukidi, went up into the mountains of New Ireland and were killed and eaten in exactly the same way. How did Fiji react to the news of the murder of Sailasa and his party of evangelists? When word came

back to Fiji and Sailasa's own brother heard of it he asked,
"Who were the missionaries killed?" and he was told, "Your
brother was one of them." Instead of being angry he bowed
his head and said, "I am going to take his place as a missionary in New Britain."

Let me tell you a story about Joeli Bulu, the long-
term Tongan missionary whom I mentioned earlier. Joeli served
for a while in the northern island of Vanua Levu and was very
much persecuted by the heathen. They stole his pigs: they
killed his chickens: they spoilt his native bread pits. The
people who were doing this said, "When we have wasted all the
property of the Christians we are going to kill and eat them."
When Joeli heard this he said to the people of the little
Christian village, "I will go and talk to them." The people
said, "Let us all go!" Joeli replied, "No! If we all go there
will be a struggle and nothing will be achieved. Let me go
alone!" He pleaded with them, but they would not listen. In
this particular island there were some 20 or 30 Christian villages that were completely wiped out by the cannibals. However this is a story of deliverance.

Joeli said to the Christians, "Let us not try to fight
them." Now, in the early hours of the morning, just before
dawn, when it was yet still dark, they heard the Fijian war
trumpets all around the village. The Fijian method of war
was to encircle a village and then to sound the trumpet, gradually drawing in and frightening the people in the enclosure
of the village. Joeli said, "All you Christians sit down on
the grass. Nobody must fight!" The trumpeters were coming
closer and closer and the sound was getting louder and louder.
Then dawn came.

Suddenly there was a war cry from the heathens and they
burst in on the village to massacre the Christians. However,
they saw them sitting peacefully on the grass in the center
of the village and they bounded up to their victims. Their
clubs were held above their heads and their spears quivered
as they came up close to the Christian party - but nothing
happened! Later they said, "A power took possession of us and
we couldn't use the club or the spear! What is this power
that Joeli Bulu has over us?"

And one of their number came forward with a whale's
tooth [This is the Fijian instrument of atonement.] and said
to Joeli, "Joeli you are a true man. We have spoiled your
bread: we have killed your chickens: we have taken your pigs:
we have treated you badly. But you are a true man, and your
God is a true God. Take this atonement and feel free to tell
us the story of your God." And Joeli told them of another
atonement that was much greater than a whale's tooth. But my

question to you today is this, "Would Joeli ever have had the opportunity of telling that message if he had not been prepared to die if God had called on him to do so?

There were other Christians in those days who did lay down their lives. One of these was Ilaija Varani, a Christain chief who maintained his position as a civil leader and fulfilled his mission as an indigenous peace-maker. After many successful missions he was struck down by a cannibal club when he was going unarmed into enemy territory to plead for peace. Someday the story of this great Christian will have to be written. Fiji never ceased to wonder at the reality of his conversion, his personal bravery, his endurance of persecution, and his ministry of reconciliation. He loved greatly and gave his life in the cause of peace.

5
Commitment

The four studies we have had up to this point form a sequence of ideas. We started by recognizing the *sovereign place of God* in the program of Christian mission and then we recognized God's use of *man as His co-worker*, "man under God" as it is sometimes called. Then, in the third place we looked at the missionary situation and saw, first Paul, and later the people in the South Pacific *penetrating the situation*. Then we took a look at the *persecution* of Christian evangelists. The way of penetration was not always easy. It was often a way of suffering.

A church isn't planted, or a church doesn't grow, unless people are converted. The idea of penetrating the situation means not only to convert men to God but also *to leave a working fellowship,* to leave a functioning church group. Do you remember that chapter in the *Book of Acts* about Ephesus? It finishes with Paul going away, but the last verses imply that he left the fellowship of the brethren behind him (Acts 20:36-38). He left a community of Christians who had demonstrated their conversion and commitment by burning their magic books - the symbol of their old pre-Christian loyalties (Acts 19:19). Now we are to examine this matter of conversion and commitment. There are two ways of dealing with this subject. Either we may consider individuals coming to Christ, or we may consider groups of people (i.e., groups of individuals) coming together as little (or big) social units, like a family, say, or a clan (cf. Acts 9:35). In either case the experience of each individual is the same and the transformation is in-individually felt.

The word *conversion* means "to turn about". We can use the word in a general way - I am converted to this belief, or

41

to that way of doing a thing. It means that once I did not
think this way, but now I do. I have "turned about" to a
different point of view. But as a theological word we mean
conversion from some pagan god or spirit to the Christian God
whom we know in Christ, by grace, through faith. We can say,
if we like, that the *not-people-of-God* have become *people-of-
God*, if I speak collectively, or if I speak individually, the
pagan man becomes *Christ's man*. This is what I mean by conversion in this book, the process of bringing men from their
old gods to God through Jesus Christ, and it is a good thing
for the convert to be able to *demonstrate* this change of heart
or change of life.

One way of demonstrating this change of heart is found
in Acts 19, in the incident mentioned above that occured at
Ephesus. Although Paul had many converts there, we are not
told very much about how they became Christian, but we are
told how some of them witnessed to the city by their declar-
ing that change of faith. Many of those converts had been
sorcerers and magicians. The record which tells how these
people demonstrated their conversion is found in v.19.

> Many of them also used curious arts brought their books
> together, and burned them before all men: and they
> counted the price of them, and found it fifty thousand
> pieces of silver.

Now, this is a great deal of money, and the number of magical
books which cost that much must have been a great many indeed.
Moreover, this huge bonfire of books must have represented *a
great movement* among the magicians and sorcerers. That is
one way of demonstrating a new way of life, a change of life.
In this chapter and especially the next one, we will be dealing with this kind of demonstration of new faith commitment
as it happened in the South Pacific.

This, then, is a study about conversion and commitment
as a process - something that goes on in the life experience
of people. I shall use a simple diagram to show what I mean
by the periods and points of the Christian experience of conversion and commitment.

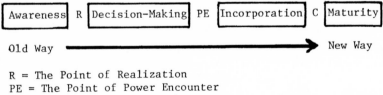

R = The Point of Realization
PE = The Point of Power Encounter
C = The Point of Consummation   Fig.4

It might be said that in the course of a man's Christian experience he passes through four periods [the blocks in the
diagram] and each one is marked off from the next one by an
experiential point. I hope the diagram may be helpful to anyone - evangelist, pastor, missionary or any other kind of
minister - whose main business in life is to lead people from
the 'old way' to the 'new way'. We may say, if you like, that
this is the journey of the soul, and we want to point out the
places where the ministry may fail or succeed. In this book,
although I am talking about missions rather than about pastor-
ing, nevertheless the experience is the same whether you are
winning someone outside your door or someone in a remote island. Only in the first stage is there very much difference.

        Let us suppose I am a missionary and I go to a place
where the people have never heard the Gospel. I am quite
strange to them, they have never heard the English language,
they have never seen a fellow with a face like mine, they
have never seen a man who dresses like me. I am a stranger,
I am a mystery to them. I am a problem because they don't
know who I am or what I am, and the same applies to the Gospel I have come to preach. They do not feel they need this
new message I bring. They say to me, "You have your God and
we have our gods. Our gods look after us when we worship
them. We make our sacrifices and they care for us." So, at
first they do not know who I am, why I am there, or what I am
doing. Now, at the church in the city people *do* know why you
are there. They know what a pastor is. They know what a
church is. But away out in many lands they do not know this,
and so I suppose the first thing those people ask about me
is, "Who is this fellow? What is he doing here? Why does he
want to live with us?" You see, they cannot put me in a slot
or category because they do not know me.

        I remember, not very long ago, going with a Melanesian
Church of England pastor to a pagan island in the Eastern Solomons where there were no Christians. Although some of the
surrounding islands had become Christian, this little island
was solidly pagan. We went out to the landing place in a
canoe, and when we came in to land on the shore the pagan
chief and his bodyguard stopped us and, pointing at me, the
chief said to the pastor, "What is he?" He didn't even ask
who is he, he said, "*What* is he?" And then he said, "Is he a
tax collector?" "Is he a member of the government?" Each
time the pastor said "No". Then the chief said, "Is he a missionary?"   I being a Methodist, and the pastor being
Church of England said "No". Then the chief asked, "Is he a
custom man?" [A man who studies customs: i.e., an anthropologist, a man who buys broken artifacts.] And the pastor
said, "He's just a Christian friend of mine." But the old

chief wasn't very happy about it at all. If I had been a
tax collector or a government servant he would have known how
to act. If I had been a missionary he would have known how
to act. But he didn't know who I was, and he didn't know
what to think about me. I was a problem.

Now when a missionary goes to a place where the name
of Jesus has never been heard he usually starts in some kind
of a position like this. That is why it makes such a difference if the Lord has opened the way, and if the field is ripe.
Before very long the people get to know you. They observe
your way of life. They see you at work. They hear what you
say. And before long they begin to say that you are a "religious man." They may think of you as a priest or a magic man.
They may even misinterpret what you say because of the image
they give you. But sooner or later, in God's time, it suddenly dawns on them that you have something to offer that they
need, and what has been slowly growing as *an awareness* suddenly becomes a *point of realization,* when they focus on something with new and significant meaning to them. Now they may
be quite wrong in their reasoning. They may be quite wrong
in their motive for coming to you. And if they are wrong in
this motive, sooner or later you have to correct that error.
But from the moment the pagan realizes the missionary has
something good for him, something he now wants, he enters this
second period of his experience.

I call this the period of decision-making. He now
knows that you have something worthwhile, and he is now asking himself, "How can I get this?" He says to himself, "This
gospel would surely be valuable to me, but do I really want
it? What kind of a price do I have to pay to get it? What
do I have to give up to become a Christian? If I become a
Christian by myself and all my family is pagan what will happen to me?" So this is the period of decision-making. The
pagan knows he wants to make the decision, but can he bring
himself to do it? Can he pay the price? After this goes on
for a certain time (it may be a matter of minutes or of years)
he makes up his mind, "Yes, I will turn my back on my old
gods and I will turn to Jesus Christ as Lord."

Now, as yet he knows very little about Jesus. He has
not as yet been taught the Gospel. He has not thought of
Jesus as his Saviour. He is still struggling against the
powers of the old religion, and he sees Jesus as "Lord of Power" who will help him to overcome the old religion. A man
who worships other gods has to throw away his gods before he
can worship Christ, and this is part of the struggle. He
says, "These are the gods of my family, or of my people. That
little god on the shelf in my house is the god of my house,

who protects the building and its residents. That stone out
there in the garden protects my garden. So if I turn to this
Jesus I have to give up all these other gods." Thus it becomes a struggle, a *power encounter*. But Jesus said, "All
power is given unto me," and so the pagan often says, "The
power of Jesus is so great, it is big enough to carry me through
all these problems and I will become a Christian." The anim-
ists of pre-Christian Fiji, in the South Pacific, had to put
their faith in Christ as a Lord of Power before they could
even be taught the theology of Jesus. Now how did the missionary know, how did the other people in the village know, that a
man had come to this point in his life?

When we have a rally of the Billy Graham type, he asks
the people to demonstrate this change of life. He invites
them to come forward. They go forward, and he has trained
workers to pray with them. But all of the congregation have
seen those who gather at the 'altar'. They have shown their
change of life by demonstrating it as an act of commitment.
So the South Pacific Islander, when he reached this point, did
not come up to the front as you would in a Billy Graham meeting, but he took that little idol off the shelf in his house
and he destroyed it or he threw it away, thereby proving to
his people it was no longer of any value to him. It was only
a *thing*. Or he may have thrown it in the river, or in the sea,
or he may have burned it. But whatever he did proved to his
family and his friends that he no longer believed in it and
that he was prepared to stake his life on Jesus. Everyone
knew that cost him something in the socioreligious system. He
needed a strong faith and great courage to be able to do that.
Like the Queen in Hawaii who worshipped the volcano goddess.
When she walked up to the top of the volcano and climbed down
into the crater just over the ledge and threw stones into the
volcano to prove to her people that she no longer feared the
fire goddess. This was a brave act and it required a strong
faith. The encounter was between the old goddess and Jesus
Christ.

Now, I have tried to diagram a process to show the series
of steps in a man's spiritual experience. A man has to go
through these steps, if he doesn't *realize* that the Gospel has
something for him then he can't go any further. If he doesn't
come to the point of *power encounter* then he never becomes a
real Christian. If he doesn't go a step further and see himself as a sinner and the Lord as a saviour, then he cannot mature properly. There is no fixed time for the length of the
periods. When the Gospel came to Tahiti the people were in
the pre-encounter stages for 16 years, but when it came to Ono
they passed out of this in a few days. Some people have been
able to make their decision in a few moments, others have taken

many years. Some people have made a decision like this but
have never really been incorporated into the church.(I shall
return to this later.) Some attend church but never grow,
because they do not become participants in the church. If I
looked back through my life I would have to say I lived all
my boyhood in this early state. I remember struggling for
quite a long time with the "idea of salvation". I remember
when I reached each of these points in my spiritual pilgrim-
age. Some people move quickly, others move slowly.

When I became a minister of a church I saw clearly
that I had people in the congregation who were what the Bible
describes as "multitudes in the valley of decision". I even
preached on that text. I found that when people could be
brought to an act of commitment in a converting experience
they went on to grow and mature; but those who made no commitment never did mature.

Let me narrate another story about John Williams, who
made that ship *The Messenger of Peace*. He had left two teachers on a little island away out in Polynesia and the chief
who had promised to look after them had not been very true to
his promise. In the first place he had really given permission for those teachers to be there just to make a profit out
of them. When John Williams came back to see how they were
getting on, the boat arrived on the Lord's Day and the chief
went on board the ship to trade. Williams said to him, "This
is the Lord's Day. No trade! I'm just about to preach a
sermon. You can sit and listen." So the chief sat down on
the deck of the ship and listened to the sermon. John Williams opened his Bible and read Isaiah 44:9-20 in which the
prophet discusses the craftsman who took the tree and shaped
an idol from its wood. Williams read the passage until he
came to this verse about the tree -

Then it becomes fuel for a man; he takes a part of it
and warms himself, he kindles a fire and bakes bread;
also he makes a god and worships it, he makes it a gra-
ven image and falls down before it. Half of it he burns
in the fire; over the half he eats flesh, he roasts meat
and is satisfied; also he warms himself and says, "Aha,
I am warm, I have seen the fire!" And the rest of it
he makes into a god, his idol; and falls down to it and
worships it; he prays to it and says, "Deliver me, for
thou art my god!"

Can you imagine what happened? Here they were on the
ship and John Williams was reading the Bible. The chief was
sitting there listening to the Bible reading. And when he
heard this verse he suddenly realized the difference between
a piece of wood, and what he thinks is a god, but which cannot

really save him. Immediately he came to the *point of realization*. He forgot he was listening to a Bible reading.   He
stamped his foot on the deck.   He jumped up and exclaimed,
"What fools we have been! We have been confusing *moa* with
noa!" Now *moa* is their word for "the sacred", and *noa* is
their word for "the profane".   So the truth that suddenly
came to him was that in this whole business of idols they were
confusing the profane with the sacred.   "That is a profane
thing and we have made it a god!" The Polynesians love those
words which have similar sounds and mean opposites, so he saw
the contrast - the *moa* and the *noa*.   The chief stopped the
Bible reading and declared, "To the day of my death I will
never again worship an idol with eyes that cannot see and
hands that cannot feel!" You see, that made all the difference in that man's life, and it came in a moment of time when
he realized that truth.   In passing, let us observe the missionary role.   A missionary should never destroy another man's
idol.   He may hope and pray the other man will destroy his
own idol.   But a missionary cannot make a man become a Christian.   He has to *make his own decision*.

We have concentrated on the point of realization. Now
let us focus on the point of power encounter. This is the
point where the new convert is actually ready to face his old
gods and demonstrate that he no longer fears them.   Remember
that we discussed the two powers, the power of evil and the
power of the Lord.   There is an account of a power encounter
in I Kings 18, where Elijah challenged the prophets of Baal
and the people sat there watching to see what would happen.
They discovered that the power of Baal was a little thing compared with the great power of the true God.   But it was a test,
a dramatic struggle between two forces.

The story is told in the Solomon Islands about a Christian evangelist who was preaching the Gospel, but the people
would not listen to him because they said, "We are afraid of
the power of our god who lives in that banyan tree."   And
every time the evangelist told them about the Lord they re-
minded him of the banyan tree with the powerful spirit in it.
And they said, "This Lord you tell us about: we cannot see
him, but we can see the banyan tree."   A banyan tree, by the
way, is a big tree that stretches out and lets down roots
from the branches to the ground.   In many countries of the
world it is a religious tree.   The old pre-Christian Fijians
used to say, "A spirit lives in the roots of the banyan tree."
These Solomon Islanders had many tales about this tree that
was so ancient that no one could tell just how much power was
attached to it.

The Christian evangelist argued, "My problem in this
place is not the people, but the demon that lives in that
tree." So he said to the people, "If you believe that the
demon in the tree is more powerful than my God, I will chop
the tree down." And this was to be a challenge to him, just
like Elijah challenged the prophets of Baal. All the people
gathered on the day he declared he would cut down the tree.
This "trial by challenge" was approved by everyone, and they
said, "If you cut down that tree you will die, but if you
don't die, we will know that your God is stronger than the
spirit in it." So everyone was nervous and excited about the
great contest.

The Christian evangelist began cutting down the tree.
Some of the people hid their faces for fear of what the spirit
would do to him and his party. But the tree was cut down and
nothing happened to the evangelist. Then he brought along
some wood from the tree and made it into a cross. He put the
cross in the ground where the banyan tree had been growing
and said, "This will be a sign to you that the symbol of the
God of power is a cross. He is not like a spirit living in
a tree or in a wooden cross. This is rather a sign of the
story of what He did for us." And he preached Christ cruci-
fied for sinful man. Then he said to the people, "If you
want a sign, the sign is there. It is the cross. But you
must not worship the cross like you worshipped the banyan tree.
It is just a reminder of what the Lord did for us."

There was a man in Fiji whose name was Varani - that
was a "name-with-a-meaning". It was an old Fijian way of saying "Frenchman". It sounds like "France" or "Frenchie". This
man was a cannibal, and he was the war chief of a little island called Viwa. He was the right-hand warrior, the captain
of the army, of the greatest cannibal chief that ever lived
in Fiji. When the cannibal chief wanted to go to war he sent
a message to this man. The king depended on him for the organization of the army. He lived on Viwa and the king lived
on another island, Bau, just nearby, and they had contact
with each other all the time. On the subordinate island,
Viwa, where Varani lived, there began to grow a little church.
There was a missionary there, and the place became the main
station where the early Fijian evangelists were trained.
They were allowed to build a church, and the work grew. Converts whose villages were destroyed by cannibals frequently
took refuge in Viwa, but Varani himself was still a cannibal
and a heathen.

Now it happened that a group of young Viwans about
13 or 14 years of age began to reason in the following manner
about their chief - "What can we do to help our young church

in this cannibal island?" And one of them said, "If our chief
was a Christian it would make all the difference in the world.
We can't do very much by ourselves, but if he was a Christian he could do so much." These boys had seen an important
missiological truth, that there are natural leaders in a society and that it is a good thing to have them won for the
Lord. So the boys decided that the best thing they could do
was to meet in the forest and pray for their chief. So, day
by day, as they were going to work, they went off into the
forest by themselves and they prayed, "Lord, save our Big
Chief, and make him a Christian." Now, that was a very practical thing that young Christians could do in that day.

Varani was a very wise man, even though he was a cannibal and a heathen. As his people became Christian one by
one and family by family, he noticed that their lives changed.
There was something about this third stage of being incorporated into the group that mystified him. When those people
came together in the fellowship he saw that their faces changed, their ethics changed, their whole way of life changed.
Something was going on in that small Christian group - that
fellowship of believers. So Varani said, "What *is* going on
in that group?" He asked, "When one of my people becomes a
Christian, what does the missionary or the evangelist do to
him?" The man he questioned replied, "Well, the first thing
that happened to me was that they gave me an alphabet and I
started to learn to read." "Read!" Varani asked, "What's
read?" "We learn letters," the man replied, "and write the
letters down, and someone else can read those letters, and a
message can be communicated in this way, even though they
cannot hear our voice." Varani said, "I'm the Chief of these
people and they can do things that I can't do!" So he went
to John Hunt, the missionary, and said, "I want to learn to
read!" Now that was unusual, because normally people became
Christians before they learned to read. This is the only case
I know, of a man who learned to read before becoming a Christian, in Fiji, in those days.

The missionary said, "Alright, I will prepare some lessons for you." Hunt spent a long time finding the most ap-
propiate texts in the Bible to teach this cannibal chief to
read. So when the first short sentence was given to Varani,
he read something like - "God is love." And as soon as he
had learned these words, he asked, "Who is God?" And then he
asked, "What is love?" And so the missionary told him about
God, and about God's way, and God's way of love. And all the
passages of Scripture that were chosen by John Hunt were the
kind of passages aimed at making Varani think about what
Christ had done for him.

One day Varani heard that there was to be a special
worship service that was not held on the regular Sunday. You
will guess what the day was. It was Good Friday. John Hunt
selected a number of texts that related to Good Friday and
the sacrifice of Christ on the cross, for sinful man. When
Varani read these passages he asked, "Is this true, that this
man died for me?" You see, he was coming to the point of
realization, and the prayers of the boys in the forest were
being answered. Then he asked, "This service - when does it
come around again?" Hunt replied, "We remember it once a
year, and it will be twelve moons before it comes round again."
Varani had now come into the period of decision-making. He had
realized the truth, but he *had not yet acted on it,* not yet
made his decision. He was in that period of decision-making.

The week went by to the Friday. For some time Varani
had been attending the Sunday services, but he had never become a follower of Christ. But on this day, when the message
of the sermon was about the work of Christ upon the cross,
Varani got up from the place where he had been sitting on the
floor and walked up to the front of the congregation, and
there he kneeled down and gave his heart to the Lord. The
Fijian phrase is: "He bowed before the Lord". So you see, he
had gone through the period of awareness, he had the point of
realization, he had gone through the period of decision-making, made his decision, and before all the people who knew
him only as a fierce cannibal he came and humbly bowed himself
before the Lord. After that he now had to be incorporated
into the little congregation.

Now, how do you bring a man who has been a great warrior chief into the Christian church and make him a Christain
worker? Some of the British missionaries wanted to persuade
him to become a Christian teacher or evangelist. They said,
"Because this man has authority and now has a Christian experience, he will be a great evangelist." And no doubt, in
time, he would have become a Fijian minister, if he had followed that path. But Varani said, "No, I am a Chief. I have
the duty of leading my people in their various work programs
and social responsibilities, and I feel that God wants me to
show them what it means to be a good Chief. I will run my
community in a new and different way. I will protect them
from war instead of leading them into war." And, as good as
his word, Ilaija Varani became the greatest peacemaker of all
Fijian history. He travelled to the very places where before
he had previously made war and laid waste the land; but now
he tried to persuade the people to give up war, and live in
peace. He is still remembered to this day as a model Christian layman, and a man of strong faith, who resisted tempta-
tion, who witnessed for Christ wherever he went. Thus was

this chief incorporated into the church.   In the end, he gave his own life on a mission of peace and died a true martyr for the faith.

This story is an account of the conversion of an individual.   It is the story of one man, a man who was born a leader of his people, who had many skills and abilities, and how he became a member of the Christian group and his life was changed.   But it wasn't always this kind of story, because of the communal nature of life in the islands.

Fig. 5

Deep-Sea Tongan Canoe of the Contact Period

6

People Movements

In the New Testament the church is conceived as a structured group or corporate entity - the building with its parts fitly framed together (Eph 2:21), the Body of Christ (Rom 12: 4; Eph 4:12; Col 1:18; I Cor 12:27, &c.), the flock of God (Eph 2:19) and so on. The first thing needed when people make a commitment to Christ is to have such a group into which they are incorporated (I John 1:3) and thereafter operate as parts of the Body - i.e., participate in the life of the church.

In the history of the spread of Christianity, the places where it has taken root are those places where Christian groups have emerged. A few individual Christians do not make a church. It takes body-life to make a church. And more often than not the strongest Christian communities have been those which became Christian as whole groups. Jesus stimulated a group at Sychar (John 3:39-42). The faith was transmitted to whole families like that of the Philippian gaoler (Acts 16:30-33). Whole villages, like Lydda and Saron, turned to the Lord (Acts 9:35). The folk who responded to God under the influence of the Holy Spirit at Pentecost were mostly linked by the social ties of being Jews of the dispersion (Acts 2:9-11,41).

The South Pacific was no exception to this rule. The Gospel spread through social units - families, lineages, tribes, occupational groups or villages. Even though every convert has to be brought personally to Christ as an individual, for the most part people have moved into Christianity in groups, and frequently the emerging churches have reflected those social structures.

In this chapter we will carry further our study of conversion and commitment, paying more special attention to the group underpinnings.

In the last chapter we considered the case of the conversion and commitment of Ilaija Varani of Viwa. We saw him
as a strong individual who dared to break away from the old
socioreligious structures and open the door for innovation.
He could only do this because he was a strong chief and wanted
the basic social system to survive. A commoner could not have
achieved this. Very few individuals could act *in spite of*
(against) the group. A leader had to carry the group with him,
and this was especially so in the days of persecution, when a
converting individual or family might be killed for their
change of faith.

It was like this in the Kingdom of Bua, as I have already described. In the graph I have drawn the pattern of the
growth of the church in Bua, with the number of Christians
along the side, and the years along the bottom. You will observe that the line went along for a long, long time, almost
horizontally, and you might think there was no growth.   But
yet some hundreds of whole villages became Christian during
those years. However, as soon as a village became Christian,
the heathen attacked it. They burned the houses and killed
the people. Sometimes they killed the men and took the women
and children away as slaves. So this period of about ten
years looks like a period of non-growth, but there were hundreds and hundreds of people who became Christian and lost
their lives. As many died as were converted.

Yet the conversion of heathen Buans to Christianity
went on. The movement was led by another Christian chief who
took the name of Esekaia when he was converted. Ra Esekaia
was the eldest son of the Paramount Chief of Bua, a notorious
cannibal, and very much against the new religion. Ra Esekaia
found that the heathen forces in the land were too strongly
arrayed against the Christians. He, himself, only survived
because of his high birth. What protection the Christians had
was because of Ra Esekaia, but he knew he could never rule the
divided kingdom if his father died and he became the ruling
chief. So he did an incredible thing. He handed over his
chiefly status and authority to his younger brother, Ra Masima, who was still a cannibal, and resigned himself to pro-
tecting the young church in Bua. Had it not been for this
no Christians would have survived. All through the persecution he held them together.

The few Christians who escaped from the countless mas-
sacres sought protection at Tiliva, a mission village across
the river from the pagan settlement of the Chief of Bua, and
here, in defiance of the persecutors, Ra Esekaia, with the
help of missionary Thomas Williams and the Christian community built a "church house" - a very fine piece of architect-
ure such as had not been seen in Fiji before, to the astonish-

ment of the heathen. Then he sent messages out to the little
pockets of Christian people all over Vanua Levu and called
them together, for the first time, to the opening of the church
at Tiliva. Ra Ezekaia spoke to these people, "Now you see
that you are not just a little handful of people, but part of
a large community with scores of little handfuls all over
the land. Be faithful to your fellowship group," he contin-
ued, "and faithful to your Lord. Sooner or later the persecution will pass and these little Christian cells will become
big churches." And meantime he worked and prayed for the conversion of his brother, and for the heathen of his land. E-
ventually Ra Masima was converted, and by this time the heathen had become so astonished at the faithfulness of the little Christian groups everywhere that in whole villages they
became Christian. You can see this on the graph. That is
another way in which a man became incorporated into the church
and became active and carried his responsibility as a Christian.

Now let me narrate a few things about the conversion
of Ratu Cakobau, the great cannibal king of Bau, whom I have
already mentioned. He was a giant man, and a terrifying man
in his heathen days. He had killed and eaten 1000 bodies before his conversion. He had an interesting lot of names and
titles: Ratu Seru Cakobau [Cakobau is archaic idiom for "Bau
is at war"], his title was Vunivalu [Root of War], his enemies called him Cikinovu [Centipede] and he claimed the title
(not always admitted by his enemies) of Tui Viti [King of
Fiji]. When he was converted he elected to be named, Epenisa
[Ebenezer]. He lived on a small island fortress known as Bau,
a mile or two across the water from Varani's Viwa, and the
coastal communities along the mainland coast opposite Bau were
his warrior clans. One might ask the question - "Who could
defy such a Chief?"

Now supposing a Paramount Chief like this wanted to become a Christian - a Chief - a man with all the authority of
the Chief - do you think he could do it as an individual? He
could not. There were many things that stopped him and limited his power. That is why Ra Esekaia gave up his status,
because he knew that no Christian leader could rule while the
kingdom was not with him.

At the time Cakobau was converted, his country was at
war, and there are three things he had to do before he could
register his conversion. He had come to the point of realization. He knew that Christianity was true. And he had come
into that period of decision-making. And for long he had been
saying, "I will become a Christian, but not yet. I've got a
few more wars to fight before I become a Christian." So here
is a man who knew what he ought to do, but put off doing it.

But as time went on, it became more and more clear to him
that he would have to give himself to the Lord. That the Lord
wanted him and he could not go on saying "No!"

Cakobau's wife had already become a Christian, and she
was witnessing to him. And then, one day, he said, "Call the
evangelist." And there in his house, with his wife and the
evangelist, he "bowed the knee" to the Lord, and told the
evangelist that at the next Sunday's worship service he would
do it in public. But he was not quite free to act as an individual like that, so he sent out a message to the people
of his family. By "family" I mean "extended family", his kin.
And this was quite a big family. He called them all together
at the chiefly house. This was a very big house called the
"Strangers' House" where some hundreds of people could meet.

Cakobau addressed all his family, "I want to become
a Christian." He wanted the approval of his family, because
he knew that if he did not have the family approval they
would just dispose of him and appoint another leader, and he
knew they could only remain strong if they were united. So
he said, "I want to become a Christian, and I want you to become Christians too." One of the members of the family, a
senior man, spoke up, saying,"Well Ratu, we approve of your
becoming a Christian, but with the political situation as it
is we do not think you should do it yet." And for the
best part of the day the family talked it over, and many of
them said, "Yes, we should all become Christians." And some
of them said, "We don't want to stop it, but we think the time
isn't ripe." It took all day, but at the end of the day they
said, "Alright, we'll let Ratu Cakobau become Christian, and
all those who want to follow him may become Christian too."

The next day he called together all the leaders of his
kingdom and said to them, "I want to become a Christian."
And the same thing happened as had happened in the family,
for another day they discussed whether or not it was safe for
Ratu Cakobau to become a Christian. And they came to the
same decision.

This decision was important, because he was still at
war and he knew that if he said, "Well, the war is over, I'm
not fighting any more," his enemy would still come down and
all the more want to fight. He had to be sure that all the
groups of his kingdom would still be loyal. So you see that
a man in a position like this is not altogether free. He
made his personal decision in his house. He talked it over
with his extended family, or kin, and he talked it over with
the leaders of the kingdom. Then on the following Sunday,
as good as his word, he came forward and bowed the knee to
the Lord in public, and about three or four hundred of his

lineage did it at the same time as he did. They did not do
so just because he did it; they did it because they too
wanted both to become Christians and maintain their social
cohesion. But everybody acted together at the one time, in
the same place, because this was the way things were done.
It was their cultural pattern for making a momentous decision like this.

    People often come to Christ in groups. Sometimes it
is a family, sometimes it is a village. In some societies
it is an age-grade - a level of people born at the same time,
a peer group company.   It may even be an occupational
group - all doing the same kind of work. There are many kinds
of groups. In the case of the Western Solomon Islands, where
people lived in a head-hunting complex, there were many slaves
that had been captured, and these slaves were kept and fat-
tened so that they could be used for a sacrifice later on.
The easiest way for a man like that to save his life was to
become a useful person. Many of them became makers of shell
money. These slaves had come from all different parts of the
islands. They spoke different languages, and were of different tribes. But the fact that they were all slaves, and that
they could all be sacrificed, and that they were all victims
there in the one place made them into a solid group. And
they all became Christians as a group, and yet each one because he wanted to do so. So although it was a group decision, it was also a multi-individual decision. They had talked
it over for some time and had reached a concensus.

    When people become Christian in this way, in families
and groups (and if you go as a missionary to some societies
this is the way you will find it there), quite often the group
becomes a little fellowship group - a church. When an individual is converted by himself, he has to be incorporated
into the church which is already there, and if there is no
church there for him, then he is in difficulties. But when
a group of people become Christians, as a group, the group
can then become a church. This is what we call "church planting" - evangelism. This church planting is culturally con-
ditioned, and the convert has to demonstrate that the old
powers no longer control him. Now let me give a few brief
illustrations to show this.

    In a part of Tahiti called Eimeo, the most feared thing
was the idol, or god. This god was made out of wood and
clothed in a dress made of coconut fibre. Now there were a
lot of these idols. One day, the priest, whose name was Patii,
said to the evangelist, "Tomorrow, I will burn my gods." And
the story went around Eimeo that Patii was going to burn his
gods. Everybody gathered together, and they were as afraid as

those people in the Solomon Islands were when the banyan tree was cut down. The priest had his assistant priest build a fire, then he took the greatest of the gods and held it up before the people. He told them that this was the god they had served so long, and he himself, as the priest, had offered sacrifices to it. But he now knew that it was a false god. He pulled off the dress and threw it into the fire, and then he threw the god in after the dress. Everyone was astonished and afraid, but the priest suffered no harm. Nothing had ever happened in that part of Tahiti before that so undermined the faith which the people had in their gods. This man had been priest of the god, so he, as priest, destroyed the god. Then the people began to ask themselves about all the little gods they had in their houses, and there began a wave of burning gods. It was a group behaviour pattern, but they all acted as individuals. This was the way it was done in that part of Tahiti, because to them the most powerful thing in their religion was their belief in the gods. But it wasn't always exactly the same.

In another part of Tahiti where the people believed in a religious system of sacred animals which were forbidden as food without certain religious rites, the King, Pomare, determined to break the food taboo and eat his sacred turtle without the heathen ritual. He did just that, and everyone in the house trembled. He invited them to join in the meal, but all were afraid. They expected the earth to open up and swallow him for such sacrilege. When nothing happened the power of the old religion was broken. The power encounter had to be at the focal point of power in the old religion - the idol, the sacred taboo, and so on.

In Fiji, the sacred thing was the holy grove, where the gods or ancestral spirits lived, and when the people wanted to turn away from their old gods they cut down the trees in the grove and built a church with the timber. If it had been the Solomon Islands it would have been the ornamented skulls and the skull houses. (Places where they put the skulls of their enemies, and built up power - the more skulls you had, the more power you had.) In Malaita I visited a certain cemetery. I saw crosses on all the graves except for one big grave made of cement, as if some giant must have been buried there. The people told me that that particular grave was full of skulls. When they turned from their old religion, (and they did so as a village, as a whole village) they took all these much feared sacred things and put them all in one grave to demonstrate that they would no longer draw on the power of their evil presence, but rely on God alone.

A friend of mine told me the story and showed me pictures of what happened in the Highlands of New Guinea when the people brought their fetishes and sacred paraphernalia and burnt them. This was the demonstration of a decision. In Western society we have to demonstrate as individuals that we have become Christians. In this kind of society the demonstration is often made as a group. And, by the way, this is not limited to the South Pacific. It happens in Africa and among American Indians and in other places. Any of you who go as missionaries to communal societies may face this kind of issue.

I have another very important thing to say about this. The missionary or the evangelist must not destroy these idols. They are not his gods. The only man who can destroy a god or a magical object is the man who worships it. In a big movement like the one in New Guinea, when a tribe of maybe as many as 6000 people demonstrates their decision together, the act is quite complex. Who destroys the gods of the tribe at large? The man with authority over that tribe - either the priest or the Chief - brings that god for destruction. But there are also gods of families. Who destroys the family gods? The head of the family. And there are also personal gods. Who destroys the personal gods? The individual whose god it is. People make their decisions in the pattern of their culture. We call this a multi-individual decision. If you go to this kind of country you will meet this kind of experience. I hope that some of you do go and are used by the Lord in this kind of evangelism.

If you do so, you will find two things, which seem to be in conflict, are both essential. On the one hand, the Lord requires a clear-cut separation from the old gods. But on the other hand, He does not want the cultural heritage to be destroyed. The people still have to live in the same kind of geographical terrain and the same environment, meet the same kind of social needs and problems. The new religion has to give them a richer experience and apply Christ to the same given situation, and anything which is wholesome should be preserved. The religious change must be genuine and total, but the social dislocation should be minimal. One of the things which should most certainly be preserved is the communal group.

Even after a church has been well established and the first generation of people who gave up paganism have died, and the new generations comprise people born in Christian homes, each new generation will have to be brought to personal commitment to Christ for itself. Although all persons will stand face to face with Christ as individuals nevertheless the registration of commitment may still be a manifest group action on a basis of family, age grade or sex units.

I recall an incident in my own experience in Fiji. I was stationed at the time in an interracial, multilinguistic, co-educational centre. We were having an integrated worship service in English, which was the one language common to the 500 or more worshippers who included folk from an Indian Mission, an agricultural station, a small market town and a sugar mill community - Fijians, Indians, Rotumans, Tongans, Samoans part-Europeans and Westerners. The Fijians and Indians came from numerous linguistic subgroups. If a "melting pot" exists anywhere, I would have said it was there. I was preaching on the idea of "being in Christ", because I was using English and the idea does not fit well into the Fijian language. I invited the congregation to commit themselves to Christ that night, and offered to meet any so-minded. After the service, some 15 or so individuals were waiting for me. As I talked with them it suddenly struck me that they were all Fijians: they were all girls: they were all between 15 and 18 years of age. Obviously the Spirit of God was working in that ethnic/sex/age-grade group. It was a group commitment, but it was also multi-individual.

All down through history God has worked through human groups. The story which began in the Acts of the Apostles still goes on today. More people have been added to the church in this way than by any other. We should recognize that the Spirit of God works in this way, and rejoice.

7
The Emergence of the Church

Let us retrace our steps for a moment. In the previous chapters we saw first how God prepared the way for the Christian mission. We looked at the missionary situation as something which had to be penetrated. Then we talked about people becoming Christian as individuals and in groups - conversion and commitment. The question now arises - what happens to people when they are converted to Christ? Surely they have to be incorporated into some kind of fellowship group. One of the exciting things about a pioneering missionary situation is the emergence of the Church. I remember reading a report written by John Hunt in early Fiji. He had been there less than 10 years, and there was one sentence which stood out powerfully. It read - "There is a Church now in Fiji." He did not mean a building. He meant a Christian community - praying, worshipping, witnessing, growing. With this in mind we turn for a moment to the Bible.

There are many ways of reading the Bible. One way is to take a book, a gospel or a letter and sit down and read it through as a whole thing. I always find that when I read a book through whole, I see a number of things I did not see when I read it section by section. If you read through the Book of Acts as a single book you will discover certain ideas in the narrative that develop as the book goes on. And one of those themes which develops in the Book of Acts is the formation of the fellowship group which becomes the Church. It is a story about missionary work. It is a story about events in the early church. It is a story about the men whom God called. But the theme that runs right through the book is that of the formation of the Church. It emerges. It grows. It develops. It matures.

61

Take the Book of Acts and follow through, selecting such references as 2:47; 5:14; 6:7; 9:31; 11:21; 14:27; 16:40; 20:7 (and no doubt there are others) and you will see what I mean. Conversion must inevitably lead to church planting. In one event after another the book says "and the church grew", or "the Lord added to the number of believers". The converts cannot mature or "grow in grace"; they cannot organize social work; they cannot plan or organize their ministry until the Church emerges.

It was so in the Bible and in the South Pacific; the same thing happened. The Lord brought the Church into existence. Often God brought people to Himself even before any missionary arrived. But as soon as there were people who believed, there came into being a fellowship group.

In the island of Tahiti the missionaries were not successful for 16 years. But the people watched and saw how the missionaries lived, and the first island 'Christians' in Tahiti were actually men who said, "These missionaries are praying people." So a number of them went away into the forest and prayed. And these were the first Christians. They were not responding to a gospel message, they were responding to the fact that they saw the missionaries were religious men, that they were praying people. These Tahitians called themselves "the praying group". Even though they knew very little about God and about Christianity, nevertheless they saw themselves as a group. They saw their own entity. They were a solid thing - the praying group.

When John Williams, whom we talked about earlier, went to Eastern Samoa (now American Samoa), there was a place there called Leone. The first time John Williams sailed into the harbour of that little place he found a group of Christians there - not just one Christian here and one over there, but a group of them. They called themselves "Sons of the Word". Williams could never find out where they got that name, because there hadn't been a teacher of Christianity there, and they didn't have the Bible. This is just another case of how God goes before and opens the way. The group had become so strong that the heathens thought they had better have group entity too, so they could distinguish themselves from the Sons of the Word. They called themselves the Sons of the Devil.

The point about this incident is that as soon as the Christians became aware of their entity or selfhood they said, "Let us bind ourselves together." As yet, they had no idea of what a church was, but before the Gospel was preached there, the group had an awareness of its selfhood. They had their name and also a symbol - a small strip of native bark cloth tied on the arm.

The same thing applied to all the island groups. Let me tell you what they did in Fiji. When a man became a Christain two things happened. First, he asked for an alphabet, because he wanted to learn to read. Then he put on a *sulu* (a cloth that goes around the loins). He said, "This is a sign of my being in the Christian group." So when you read the letters and writings of the early church in Fiji you meet this phrase, "He put on the sulu." That is idomatic, it means "This man has confessed Jesus." But the important thing is that it was a sign of being incorporated into the fellowship group. Before these people were Christian they belonged to the pagan group. When you convert a man you cannot leave him in a vacuum. He has to belong to something, and he has to be happy in what he belongs to. So that is why the third of those periods in the diagram of growing Christian experience is *Incorporation*. A man has to be in a group. He has to feel he *belongs* to the group. He has to feel that he has a work to do and people to relate to in the group, he has to be a participator.

I have in my possession a missionary journal (diary) of a man who lived in Fiji in the 1860s. He describes in his narrative how he visited a "Christian village" here and a "heathen village" there. This kind of differentiation runs through the journal and shows that he lived in a period of history when the heathen villages were becoming Christian. In the early part of the diary there are many more references to heathen villages than to Christian villages, but near the end there are more references to Christian villages than to heathen villages. So I know that when I say the church was spreading, there were villages that were becoming completely Christian all along the line.

This is very like what we find in the Book of Acts. As the story goes on the church grows and it matures. And when we read further than the Book of Acts and get into the letters of Paul, we find that those churches must have been quite sophisticated to get that kind of letter. And this is all like what happened in the South Pacific. When God sent his missionaries to work there, the church grew, it developed, it matured.

Now, I want to demonstrate how a church grows. I am going to use another diagram which I will break into three parts. I am going to look at the church from three different angles. I am going to say that a church grows quantitatively, that it grows qualitatively, and that it also grows organically.

What do I mean? I mean that a church grows quantitatively when it grows in numbers. Men are converted and incorporated into the church, and it gets bigger and bigger. But it is not enough to grow in size alone. If we bring into

the church all kinds of people with all kinds of wrong motives,
that would not be good quantitative growth.

So we have a second kind of growth which I am calling
'qualitative growth'. This is one that focuses on the inner
life of man. He grows in faith. He develops an ethic. He
lives the Christian life. He helps those in need. He wit-
nesses to those who do not know the gospel. As the Bible says,
he "grows in grace". So if we have a church that grows in
numbers and also grows in quality - in its inner life - that
is good growth.

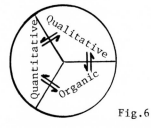

Fig.6

And then, at the same time a church has to grow organically. It grows like an organism - just as a growing baby
develops its arms, its legs, its head, and so on. In the same
way the church grows and develops new organs - an organ for
prayer, an organ for worshipping, an organ for teaching, and
so forth. A church has to grow in its structure as well as
in its numbers and in its quality. And it is important that
it should grow in every dimension.

Now, this diagram is an abstraction. It is something
"in my mind", an analysis, so that I can visualize these different dimensions. I do not mean that the church has three
compartments that you can put off separately by themselves.
There is a current going from one to another, going backwards
and forwards (⮀). All these parts relate to each other.
They cannot be separated one from the other. Only in my mind,
when I want to think about it, can I separate them into sec-
tions like this. And the proper term for this is *dynamic
equilibrium*.

Now, the above diagram shows the nature of a growing
church at a *point in time*. In reality the church lives on,
of course, *through time*. The situation is really like this
(Fig.7), if you think of, say, three generations -

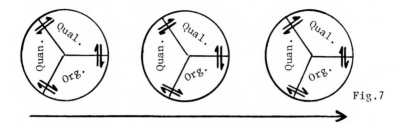

Fig.7

I call this the *continuity* of church growth. Let me explain in more detail what I mean by growth "through time". You
really cannot measure growth at a point of time. But a church,
if alive, goes on and on. It was so in the Bible and it is so
in the islands.

It started in the Pacific with men and women who gave up
their idols and became Christian. Then before long, another
generation arose - their sons who had never worshipped idols or
fetishes, or who had never been cannibals, but were born in
Christian homes. Can a man live on the spiritual experience of
his father, or must he come to the Lord for himself?

So there are two generations. And a church that is
strong and faithful in one generation may "fall from grace" in
another generation. (Remember Ephesus, Rev 2:4-5). And then,
still another generation comes on, so that the church goes on
and on. I call this "the continuity of the church." Remember
this. There are three ways in which a church grows. Those
three ways must be in equilibrium. They must all grow together.
And it must go on and on, generation after generation. This is
my theory of church growth. The important part about the continuity of the growing church is that there must be a revival
of some kind in each generation.

Now I will go back and take another look at these three
different kinds of growth. First of all, I want to discuss
a church growing in size - growing quantitatively. Let us look
at the graph below. The number of members are shown along the
side. The years are shown along the bottom of the graph. A
common graph that we meet when people come into a church by way
of a people movement is like the one depicted on the next page.

In Fiji there was usually first a period of little growth,
and what there was comprised a few individual conversions (a).
Then there was a period of very rapid growth (b). I am giving
you the statistics and graphs of the church that came in the
island of Bau, the island where the cannibal king, Cakobau, lived.
It took eight years for these people to be incorporated into
the Church. The individual conversions really go back before
1854 ('a'), but the big movement began that year ('b').

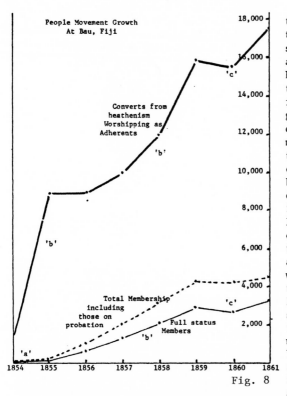

People Movement Growth
At Bau, Fiji

Converts from
heathenism
Worshipping as
Adherents

'b'

'b'

Total Membership
including
those on
probation

Full status
Members

'b'

'a'

'c'

'c'

18,000
16,000
14,000
12,000
10,000
8,000
6,000
4,000
2,000

1854   1855   1856   1857   1858   1859   1860   1861

Fig. 8

The graph covers the eight years of the movement which swept the islands and villages in the Kingdom of Bau. On the next page there is another kind of graph which shows a cross section of the movement in the third year after the conversion of Cakobau (1856-57). Each double column stands for a village or island. The left side of the column shows the number who were attending Christian worship in 1856 and the right side in 1857. So the graph shows the distribution of a people movement in process. You will notice that some places had followed the chief and others had not. Cakobau had not commanded his followers to become Christian. He said, "If you wish to become Christian you are free to do so." The subject islands had been ready to do so for some time, and certain social units in Bau itself; but the coastal villages and warrior clans were not yet ready. However by comparing the two sides of the double columns we observe that movement was beginning.

The graph of the 1856-57 cross-section (Fig.9) shows that a people movement over a large area of political control will probably comprise a number of smaller group movements with a local, or kinship, or occupational homogeneity. It shows that the group decision-making powers in the matter of religion lay, not with the paramount chief of the political kingdom, but within the domestic structures. If you are studying church growth statistics you may find that sometimes the graphs of these movements seem to 'run out' or plateau, when you know that only part of the community has been won for Christ. It is important to understand that the large community unit comprises many smaller ones, and we need to find a bridge of some kind from one to another.

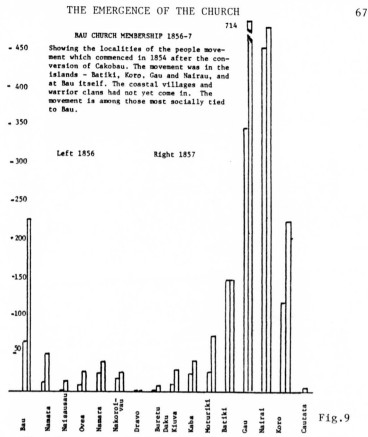

BAU CHURCH MEMBERSHIP 1856-7

Showing the localities of the people movement which commenced in 1854 after the conversion of Cakobau. The movement was in the
islands - Batiki, Koro, Gau and Nairau, and
at Bau itself. The coastal villages and
warrior clans had not yet come in. The
movement is among those most socially tied
to Bau.

Left 1856   Right 1857

Fig.9

When I went to the Solomon Islands I found an island
where half the people were Christian and half were pagan. The
former had been Christian for twenty years. So I asked an old
man, "What is your word for 'family'?" He replied, "We have
three words. We have a family of people who live in my house.
[He gave me the word.] We have another family which includes
them and also my family and their wives and children. That is
on my side, the father's side. And then there is another and
larger family which also includes those on the mother's side."
This added up to a large company, so I asked, "Who are the
Christians in this village?" He replied, "My household and
all on my side of the family." "And who are the heathen?" I
enquired. He answered, "They are my wife's side of the family."
So I asked him if he wanted a divided family, and of course he
did not. I asked if he thought he had a Christian responsibility to bring his wife's side of the family into the church. He
agreed that he did. To go back to Bau, Fiji - the graph illus-
trated above demonstrates how large-scale people movements are
comprised of many small ones and evangelism must be pressed
until all are won.

Bure of Na Vata-ni-Tawake, Mbau

This illustration is taken from a print which dates back to the actual time of the conversion moment described in this chapter. The building depicted is the sacred heathen assembly-house at Bau. A cannibal ceremony is being performed. A victim taken prisoner in war has just been killed on the killing-stone. These ceremonies ceased on Bau in 1854, which is about the date of this print.   Fig. 10

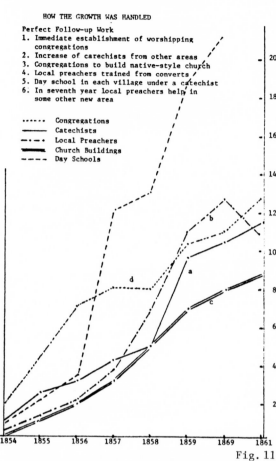

HOW THE GROWTH WAS HANDLED

Perfect Follow-up Work
1. Immediate establishment of worshipping
   congregations
2. Increase of catechists from other areas
3. Congregations to build native-style church
4. Local preachers trained from converts
5. Day school in each village under a catechist
6. In seventh year local preachers help in
   some other new area

...... Congregations
——— Catechists
—·—· Local Preachers
▬▬▬ Church Buildings
———— Day Schools

Fig. 11

The purpose of Fig. 11 is to show how the church develops organically. The graph covers the same community as Figs. 8 and 9, and the same years. An army of catechists (a) emerged. As the years went by each Christianized area was expected to produce its own leaders. The catechist built up the converts in faith, prayer, worship and Bible study. This is the qualitative growth of the church.

Line 'b' shows people emerging in congregations with spiritual gifts for articulating the faith in prayer and preaching. Some of these are soon accredited as local (lay) preachers, so that services are always possible in every small village. Usually men served first for a while as prayer leaders, then as lay preachers and finally some would become catechists, or full status ministers. Thus the functioning of the Christian fellowship led to the development of the spiritual gifts of its members (See Fig. 12).

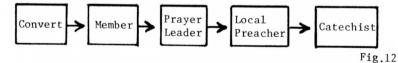

Fig. 12

Sometimes there were local preachers who cared for the work of God in small villages - a status between those of local preacher and catechist.

Line 'c' represents the number of indigenous church buildings. By "indigenous" I mean they were built from local material by the local congregation. There were no foreign buildings in these villages in those years before the "Cotton Boom" in the islands. The emergence of physical church buildings indicates the number of worshipping congregations and demonstrates the organic growth of the church. This is also supported by line 'd' which indicates the sunday schools associated with the congregations.

Now examine the two graphs (Fig. 8 and 11). You have before you the statistics of the people in the worshipping congregation (Fig.8), and the organic structures (Fig.11). The scales of the two graphs relate at 100:1 - that is, one congregational group (in Fig.11) would average about 100 persons (Fig.8). Every group of 100 worshippers had its building, sunday school, teacher and preachers, with two services each Sunday, prayer meetings, class meetings. Notice how the graphs follow the same pattern, showing how these features developed simultaneously - quantitative, qualitative and organic growth went on together. Within two years of a people-movement the community had a fully organized, practising congregation with its own building and leaders.

Moreover, if you ask why the line of local preachers drops in the later years, the answer is clear - the Church in this area had now begun to send its local preachers out as evangelists into new areas which were opening up to the Gospel. The emergence of missionary outreach in this kind of situation is a mark of growing maturity. This is what happened in the kingdom of the greatest cannibal king of Fijian history after he became Christian. Once enthusiastic cannibals, they now became enthusiastic Christians.

Now I want to say a few things about organic growth, because a church really cannot grow qualitatively if it does not grow organically.

The first picture I know of organic growth in the Church is found in the Book of Acts, in Chapter 6. This is an account of a problem that developed in the early Church. The Christians began to quarrel about the priority of *mission* and *social service*. The apostles were "preaching the Word," and one group in the church felt neglected in the ministration. For a moment it almost threatened to divide the early church. But the Christian group did the right thing. They got together and began to talk things over. They said, "Certainly it is right that we should preach the Gospel, and we must not let other things imperil that. But it is also right that we attend to the needs of the people. We must not neglect that. How do we solve this problem?

The assembly made a decision. "We will leave the
apostles to their work, so they can be true to their calling.
And we will appoint a new kind of worker to deal with this
other task," they said. This process is known as *role-creation*.
And this is how the deacon came into the church. He was not
there at the beginning. He came into being because the church
saw a social need that had to be attended to.

When you read Acts Chapter 6, you will find that there
was even an ethnic question in that situation. There was a
little racial tension in that church. And when they appointed deacons, they recognized that problem. Look at the names
of the men selected as deacons and you will see some ethnic
diversity. And one of them was a proselyte to represent the
little proselyte group in that church. What Acts 6 says to
me is that if you have a church community that is multi-
racial or comprises various social groups, you had better minister to each group in it. This is true for the mixed congregation in an urban situation, an industrial area, a planta-
tion or anywhere else where mixed ethnic groups or age groups
are collected together.

When in our missionary work we go to other lands or
tribes where people organize their social life differently
from us and have different lifestyles, we must recognize those
differences. We must recognize that other lifestyles may still
be used to the glory of God. I do not mean we should compro-
mise the Gospel - no, certainly not! But we do need to adapt
ourselves to the lifestyle of those to whom we go with the
Gospel - if we are to obtain a hearing, and to communicate.

Thus, for example, when the first missionaries arrived in Fiji they found a people with a system of communication very different from that which they had known in England.
It involved the notion of approaching people through the
medium of the herald (*mata ni vanua*). The missionaries accepted this system and learned to work within it, and it became one of the strengths of their communication. You will
remember that they had found a Fijian, a small chief from
Vulaga, who was also a dancing master (*dau-ni-vucu*), in Tonga.
He had been converted there and travelled with them to Fiji
and opened the door to the Chief of Lakeba, Tui Nayau. He
served as herald for them. When the church emerged in Fiji,
this kind of person had an established role. He is the steward (*tuirara*) in the congregation, the go-between (*mata*) for
the missionary and people, the lay representative (*mata tu-
raga*) for central synods and conferences. The whole social
structure functions on the operation of this concept and the
Church reflects this social organization. The most effective evangelistic itineration is invariably that in which the

evangelist follows the herald who opens the way, as it were,
for his message. I can say this from my own experience. When
the church accepted that indigenous approach it was growing
organically.

Another way in which the church grew organically was
by the creation of a native ministry. It was the fifteenth
year of the mission when the first South Pacific islander was
ordained as a full Christian minister. The history of the
development of the Fijian ministry is a wonderful story, and
the Fijian Church today has about 170 ordained ministers who
care for the spiritual life of the congregations. This is
organic growth, because the ministry increased in number as
the church needed it.

For five years I was the Principal of the Theological
Institution in Fiji. I was there at a time of change, a time
of transition. We had to train men for two kinds of ministry.
There was one kind of ministry in the growing town, the urban
setting, and there was another kind of ministry in the rural
area where the people were very much more traditional in their
life pattern. And we felt that we needed two kinds of minister. For ten years the church looked at this particular problem and was flexible, introducing new structures to deal with
the new problems it was meeting at the time. This is an example of organic adjustment to changing times. I wish I had
more time to deal with this, because it is a subject very close
to my heart.

Organic growth is also seen in the development of the
financial patterns of the church. The mission in Fiji planted
a church from the beginning. And although the missionary was
paid from his Board in his own country, the church itself received little financial help from overseas. The people were
taught to carry their church responsibilities when they became
Christians. You can only do this if you use native buildings.
The people said, "This is the kind of house we live in. This
is the kind of church we will build, but we will make it bigger and better." Of course, at first they did not use money.
The early lists of collections that were taken are large sheets
of paper with vertical columns. In the first column they wrote
the names of the family groups in the congregation. We will
say, the household of John, the household of Thomas, the
household of Henry, and so on. Then, instead of dollars or
shillings, they headed the 'money' columns - yams, fans, mats,
tapa cloth, dalo (taro) and so on. This was the first kind of
'financial' statement the Fijian Church kept. They paid their
ministers in mats, tapa cloth, fans and food, because these
were wealth in those days. If the missionary wanted to pay the
people, say, for helping to build a missionary's house, he would

pay for the work with axes, knives, fish-hooks, or perhaps a
New Testament. It was quite a few years before a true money
column appeared in the statements.

Now I want to take a look at the aspect of the qualitative growth of the emerging church. The first thing a convert asked for was a printed alphabet. As soon as a man became Christian he wanted to read. He wanted to know how to
use the Scriptures and the Catechism. (I shall return to the
Bible in a later chapter.) The Fijian people always had their
own forms of music. Every public occasion had its chanting.
In the Christian Church a hymnody soon developed. There was
a fine collection of hymns at an early date. John Hunt and
Richard Lyth had prepared a hymn book based on scriptural theology but using native tunes, and these were used for many
years. As time went by many fine Christian hymns were com-
posed by local people - Inoke Buadromo, Josefa Raitilava,
Lolohea Ratu, Mitiani Volau, P.E. Tatawaqa, Mosese Buadromo,
Fereti Naceba, Etoni Rarodro, Mitieli Karawa and others -
which shows how indigenous the hymnody became.

Another hymn they used in worship was the *Te Deum*.
This hymn came from away back in European history, supposedly,
from a man called Ambrose, but it is a hymn about the World
Church, and the Church Eternal, because all those who died in
the Faith are mentioned in it too. This was set to a Fijian
tune, and the Fijians really took this hymn to their hearts.
It was used whenever they had a Pentecostal outpouring of the
Holy Spirit. If they were in, let's say, a prayer meeting,
or a baptismal service, and if the people broke down in the
enthusiastic Pentecostal type of service, the whole congregation would burst into this hymn. It was a great thing to hear,
and I have a description of this by an English sea captain who
happened to call at the village and witnessed it.

Another thing that was used to develop the religious
life of the people was the chant. The Fijians used the chant
long before they became Christian. They used to chant the
stories of their heroes, and when they became Christian they
preserved this form of music. The passages of Scripture
which are lyrical and poetical in their form, suit this kind
of chanting very well. The chanting was led by the women,
and the leader of the group was not the person with the finest
voice, but often the oldest woman - oldest in years and oldest in the Faith. They would chant all the great poetic passages of Scripture - the story of creation, the story of the
building of the temple, the story of the deluge, stories of
the life and work of Christ, the story of the new Jerusalem
and many others. These passages were naturally suited to
Fijian poetic chanting. The congregation participated and

learned the passages by heart. And this was another way the
church grew in its religious life and faith, at the same time
as it grew in its organization and in its numbers.

Let me add here an experience of chanting which I myself had, because it will show you how a Fijian minister used
the women's chant in his worship service. We were at a great
meeting where hundreds of people had gathered in the biggest
church building in the area. It was a huge congregation, and
some hundreds of people were outside at the windows and doors,
looking in. The preacher that night was an old Fijian, Ratu
Nacanieli Mataika. He was retiring, and this was his last
sermon at one of these meetings. He was very concerned about
the young people – at the way they were wandering away from
the true path. So, before we went into the church, he called
in the old lady who was the leader of the chanting group and
told her what he wanted her to do. And this is what happened.
He preached his sermon, and it was indeed a powerful sermon
on "the Sin of Absalom," who turned against his father. When
he came to the end of his sermon, he gave a sign to the women
who were sitting together in the centre of the church, and
they stood up and chanted in Fijian style, David's lament over
Absalom. I do not remember hearing a more effective finish
to a sermon on that text.

The people were using their own institution, their
own mechanism. There was nothing foreign about it. It was
thoroughly Jewish, and it was thoroughly Fijian. That huge
congregation was still, and the service ended in dead silence.
Those women had preached an impressive sermon in their own
cultural form. What I want to come out of this study is that
an indigenous church *can* be planted from the beginning, if
those of you who are missionaries are sensitive to the feel-
ings and the institutions of the people.

8

The Ministry of the Word

We have been dealing with the penetration of the pagan or heathen world, the formation of groups of Christian converts into churches; and we have called this process the "emergence of the Church." We have seen how the churches grow in quantity, quality and organic entity.

As we take a hard look at the way the Church emerged we find there are a number of special themes in which we can detect this process of growth going on. In this chapter I want to look at one of those themes - namely, the "Ministry of the Word."

Of course, this is itself a biblical theme. I mean it is found both in the Old and New Testaments. In the Old Testament no one did more for the worship of the Lord than the psalmist, David. He expressed his faith that for a young man to keep pure and guard his heart from sin, he had to hide God's word in his heart, and learn its meaning for him, and meditate upon it and delight in it (Psa 119:9-16). Likewise, in New Testament times did not Paul say very much the same thing to Timothy, carrying it a step further to relate it to the saving work of Christ (2 Tim 3:14-17)? I think that we may argue from the frequency of references to the ministry of God to men and women through His Word in Scripture that as a Church emerges the ministry of the Word is expected.

The translation of Scripture becomes an urgent priority as soon as the evangelists have mastered the language adequately enough for accurate translation. Of course they should not translate until they have mastered the language. Some, in their zeal, have done this with disastrous results. But

sometimes evangelists have been too timid to translate the
holy Word of God, with equally tragic results.

I know one area in the islands where the missionaries
lived for many years. They had been there for 30 years before starting to translate the Bible. They knew the language
well and used it for purposes of trade, but they "feared" to
translate the Bible. Thousands were enquiring about Christianity and there was no vernacular Bible to give them. I
know another place where after 50 years they still had no
Bible. In both places the Christian instruction and nurture
was much more inferior than it might have been.

By way of contrast let me return again to Fiji where
the missionaries not only set out to learn the language but
to translate the Word of God into it, as well as hymns, catechisms, Bible studies and simple biblical discussions. When
the people movement came they had all the spiritual equipment
to handle it. Let me tell you what they did.

Josua Mateinaniu, whom I have mentioned as coming with
the first missionaries to Fiji (Cross and Cargill), had helped
them prepare the sounds, or letters, of the Fijian alphabet.
They had a printing press in Tonga and brought elementary
material with them.

There is a very interesting diary in New Zealand,
which I have read. It is a big book with the handwriting of
a missionary to Tonga, called William Woon, in it. William
Woon was the printer in Tonga, and he was responsible for
printing the early Bible portions, and the texts that they had,
the catechism questions and answers, and the hymnbooks they
were using. In his diary he tells the story of the Tongan
Great Awakening, and it is a very exciting story; but he sees
it with the eyes of a printer who has to print the Scripture
passages for the spiritual nourishment of these people who
were becoming Christian.

In 1838, the Lord sent two printers to Fiji, with
another printing press. Their names were Calvert and Jagger.
They were both ordained ministers as well as printers. So
you see how the Lord provided the right kind of men in this
mission field for the production of the Scriptures. Not
only did He provide the printers and the printing presses; He
also provided the Island informants to help the missionaries
translate. Mateinaniu was not the only one. There was another whose name was Noah. So there you have printers, translators and informants. This is a beautiful example of team-
work in the advancement of the Gospel. The missionaries
could not have done it without the informants; and when they
had done the translation it was of no value until it had been

printed, and could be circulated. So this is a cooperative
work of a team; and the way in which the Lord brought these
men together is a very remarkable happening.

Now let me tell you something about the two missionaries who came from Tonga, the first two missionaries for
whom Mateinaniu was the herald. One of them was David Cargill,
and the other's name was William Cross. As a linguist, Cargill was a real scholar. Besides his theological training,
he had an M.A. in languages. In those days very few missionaries had these degrees. Cargill had a great desire to bring
together a vocabulary (a dictionary if you like), of all the
words he could collect. He sat and talked with people, and
asked them how to put a sentence together. So he learned the
structure and the grammar of the language by using many island informants.

As a translator, he was a purist. He wanted a translation exactly right, word for word. That method is not so
popular among linguists today, but one of the wonderful things
about God is the way He disciplines us. God sent along the
other man, William Cross. The most important thing to Cross
was not the precise word but the meaning of the passage. So
his translations were very free, but the people who heard
them loved them. Sometimes Cross used to make Cargill angry
because of these free translations. But Cross worked in his
own way. He would take a Bible passage - maybe a parable or
a story of Jesus' miracles, (at first they were the narrative
passages rather than the difficult teaching passages) - and he
would read the passage over four or five times, until every
detail was in his mind, then he would put the Bible aside,
take a sheet of paper and begin to write. He would imagine
that he was narrating the story to a Fijian child. He wrote
down the story and read it through four or five times, until
he had an idiomatic account in very simple Fijian.

Then he would call in his recent converts who had
just learned to read, and he would give each a copy of this
story from the Bible. Then he would say, "Now, I want you to
go into a heathen village. And when you familiarize yourself
with this story, I want you to tell it to the heathen people."
At this time most of the country was still heathen. These
people who were just young Christians (only a few weeks old,
and had just learned to read and that is all), went out into
the villages, five, ten, twenty miles away. And at night
time, when the people had finished their work, and were gathered together in the big house, a Christian would say, "Here's
a story I got from the missionary down on the coast."   And
so these stories Cross had translated were carried by Fijians,
only recently converted, into all parts of the country.

Before very long, an interesting thing happened. It would always happen. The Chief of the place where one of these men had gone would become curious about the Gospel. He would say to himself, "These are good stories." Then he would ask the convert if there were any more of them. And the convert would say, "These are out of the Christian Bible, and there are many of them." Invariably the Chief would call his herald and send him down to the mission station to say, "We want to hear more about this Gospel." And this is the way many many villages were opened up to the Gospel in the early days. This is what I call "the ministry of the Word," because God was using these young converts as His ministers to diffuse His word.

Now, when the mission started in the Fiji Islands, each missionary began to learn the language or dialect of the people where he lived. They were all beginning to translate, and once a year they used to come together at the District Meeting and discuss the translation work they were doing. You see, translation work was *planned from the very beginning.*

Then after eight years it became quite apparent that some missionaries were good translators, and some were not. Then some missionary translators had better informants than others. And they said, "Surely God has given different gifts to each of us." And in this committee meeting on the eighth year, they decided that they would concentrate on one Fijian language only, and bring the best of the missionary translators and the best of the informants together to produce a really good translation of the Bible. And they chose John Hunt as the translator and Noah the main informant, and the Bauan language as the medium. This was the language of a very powerful kingdom, a kingdom with hundreds of huge canoes. Many of these would actually carry hundreds of people. Some were bigger than Captain Cook's ship that sailed the Pacific not long before. They sailed all over the Fiji Group, and the Bauan language was the most widely known.

In this language, Hunt and Noah set out to give Fiji a good translation of the New Testament. Five years later the Fijian New Testament was completed in the Bauan language. It was actually printed and in the hands of the people in the 13th year of the mission - a beautiful translation, and quite idiomatic.

Now let me tell you something about John Hunt. Hunt had come from England. He had started his life as a ploughboy, a farmer. But he was such a clumsy farmer that everyone laughed at him. But the Lord did not want him as a farmer. He became a great evangelist. He was the first Wesleyan in Britain to be given a theological training before going to the

mission field. He surprised all his teachers with his skill
in the biblical languages.

Most of the translations of the Bible that were done
on the mission field in this period of history were translations of the Authorized Version, but John Hunt worked from
the Greek New Testament. And so much of the beauty of the
Greek New Testament is found in the early Fijian version.

Hunt was as great an evangelist as he was a good linguist, and the Lord brought him out to Fiji. I have read his
diary, and what a wonderful story it is! He tells how, in his
early days as a missionary in Fiji, he had three great desires.
We might say God filled his heart with three passions. The
first of these was to translate the Scriptures into Fijian.
The second was to raise up a group of men who were trained to
use the Scriptures for preaching. And the third was to take
the Christian converts further in their Christian experience
to a life of sanctification.

At this point I am concerned with the first great
desire, and I will just mention the second. John Hunt gathered around him a large group of Fijian evangelists and trained them in the art of biblical preaching, and biblical witness.
He wrote a book called *Short Sermons*, in Fijian. They were
indeed very short sermons. There was about one page only,
per sermon, not long sermons like we preach. He gave only the
major points. Hunt did not want to make his men preach like
he did. He did not want them to become western preachers,
but he did want them to preach the biblical truth. So he it
was, John Hunt, who taught them to compose sermons, to study
the context and to make three or four points. Every page of
his book had a sermon outline like this. Then he would say
to the young men, "Here is the book, take it and preach these
sermons, but give to the people what the Lord has given unto
you in your own way. These are the bones. Put on the flesh
yourselves from your own experience." And the preachers
trained by John Hunt were powerful preachers, and they loved
him because he loved his Lord.

Now I must tell you one other chain of events in the
romance of the Fijian New Testament. You know that when a
book is prepared, not only does it have to be written and
printed, and the pages all brought together, but it has to be
bound together, as one thing. Covers have to be made, and
the pages have to be sewn in together. For this we need what
we call a bookbinder. Bookbinding is a slow and tedious task.
Of course, the two printers knew how to do it, but they had so
much work to do with the printing that they did not have time
to bind their books. But once again the Lord was in this work
and I want to tell you how He bound the Bible.

Far away in the country of France there lived a young
man in a Huguenot home. These French Protestants often lived a severe lifestyle and before long this young man got 'fed
up' with the discipline of his parents, and he decided to run
away from home. His name was Edouard Martin, and he fled
away to America where he fell into all kinds of sin. Before
long the police were out hunting for him and they nearly
caught him. He escaped by running down to the port and getting on a ship. . That ship was a whaler. It sailed down
around Cape Horn at the southern tip of South America and up
into the whaling area in the Pacific. Then the vessel sailed
into the Fiji Islands where it was caught in a terrible hurricane, and was wrecked on the reef of an island near Vanua
Levu. These were cannibal times when the church was just beginning to grow in Fiji. The cannibals of Fiji always said
that when a ship was wrecked, it was a gift of the gods to
them - to put the men in the oven. After a struggle, Martin
miraculously got from the wreck to the shore; but no sooner
had he reached the shore than he saw a huge number of Fijians
armed with clubs and spears running towards him. So he ran
into the forest and tried to get as far away from that village
as he could. As he had no food, he was getting weaker and
weaker. Then he saw a little house and a light. Very timidly
he approached the house, and he found it was the home of a
missionary. (That missionary was David Hazlewood, who later
finished the translation of the Old Testament). Hazlewood
took him in, fed him and talked with him. And Hazlewood argued with the young man that he was really afraid of his own
sin. It was his own love of sin that had made him run away
from home in the first place. It was because of his sin in
America that the police wanted him. And he really wasn't
running away from cannibals, he was afraid to die because he
knew that he was a sinner. And Edouard Martin knew deep down
in his heart that this was right. He would gladly have gone
back to his home in France, but he was on the opposite side
of the world.

David Hazlewood was working on a Fijian Dictionary,
and some of the pages were being printed, so he was glad to
have Martin there to help him with the proof-reading. And
Hazlewood led Martin to the Lord; and he became a Christian.
Then Hazlewood took him to the printing shop at Viwa, where
James Calvert taught him how to bind books. And that was the
man who bound the first Fijian New Testaments! See how the
Lord brought another man to the team! A short time after
that, Edouard Martin made a trip to New Zealand, and found
a wife. Then he went back to Fiji and served the mission there
for 14 years. He had had no theological training at all. He
was just a lay missionary, but he became a great evangelist,
and it was very exciting to me, the last time I was in New
Zealand, to see a letter written in his handwriting.

These are just some of the stories about how the Fijians got their New Testament. It is true that there were men like James Calvert, printer, and John Hunt, translator, who were historically important and were used by the Lord in the preparation of this book, but it wasn't enough just to have a Bible. The Bible had to be diffused, the people had to read it, and somebody had to teach it. The printing of the Bible is not the end of the story, it is only the beginning. Down through the history of this Church the Bible has been through about a dozen different revisions, and every time something has been improved, and now it is a very good translation. More recently, Fijian biblical scholars themselves have been working on a contemporary version.

John Hunt died in 1848. He had only translated a small portion of the Old Testament and his work was taken over by David Hazelwood, whom I mentioned earlier in this chapter. Hazelwood was a brilliant linguist, perhaps the most brilliant of them all. And that is another story - how he translated the Old Testament. A year after the completion of that work, he also died. Both of these men died young, each in his 36th year. Each had served the Lord in Fiji for ten years, and they crammed more into those ten years than most of us do in a lifetime.

Now that the Fijian people had their New Testament and their Bible, what else had to be printed to promote the growth of the Church? They had taught the people how to read, and they gave them a number of other things to read. For the school they produced arithmetic books, and geographies and histories. They even produced a textbook for teacher training.

And then for the life of the Church they produced other kinds of printed books. First of all there were hymnbooks. A hymnbook of 48 hymns came out very early in the story of the Church. And then there were some catechisms. These were prepared in the very early period, and a little later, when they had their own preachers, teachers and pastors, they began to produce literature for use in teaching the preachers. They had small books on Theology, on Biblical Introduction, and on Homiletics. And there was a very fine "Confession of the Faith," or theology of what the true Christian believes.

They also produced an edition of the Bible with very large print for the old people to read. And these Bibles have been handed down through the years. Time after time, on my journeys into the mountain villages to preach, I would see some old person with this huge Bible on the floor in front of him, nearly blind, yet able to read the very big letters. And then another version was produced which had reference columns

in it. They call it *Ai Vola Tabu Vakaidusidusi* which means
the "Pointer Bible". The pointer finger is the *dusidusi*.

What I am trying to say here is that the early Church
in Fiji was not satisfied with just producing a Bible. She
produced the large print version for the old people to read,
and the Reference Bible for the preachers to use, and is now
producing one for the younger generation. So I have always
admired the Fijian Church, because she didn't sit down when
the Bible was printed, she produced a Bible for each kind of
participant among her members.

Another printing program was that of membership tickets. In the Fijian Church each member gets a ticket every
quarter. This ticket has the member's name on it and the
minister initials it. This means that this person is a member in good standing. Underneath the members name there is
a text out of the Bible. This is a special text for the
quarter. On the first Sunday in the quarter the tickets are
given out to all the members at the church service, and the
minister preaches a sermon on the text on the ticket. Most
of the members I have seen, use the ticket as a bookmark in
the Bible. And every now and then they see that ticket and
read the text, and remember the special sermon for the quarter.

Today there is much printing being done in Fiji, both
religious and secular material. There are also Fijian news-
papers, but it was the Church that taught these people to
read. A number of novels have been translated into Fijian,
but no book has so much influenced the Fijian people (apart
from the Bible itself) as *Pilgrim's Progress*. The Fijians
really took that book to their hearts, and I know many people
who have been led to read the Bible because they have first
been challenged by *Pilgrim's Progress*.

Now the story of the Fijian Church to this time is a
very long one. It has gone through some periods when it was
very much alive, and some periods when it was not so much
alive, and in each of the live periods of the Church, signif-
icantly, there has been a lot of book publication. When I
was in Fiji I was involved in one of these programs, during
the war, and after the war. And I myself have written a number of books in Fijian. But look at the kind of books I
wrote. One was a prayer manual, because I found that the
prayers of the Fijian people, though they covered the whole
wide world, were always the same. So I wrote a book, *Let us
Pray*, of about 120 pages. On every page I set down a different way to pray and suggested a different Bible passage to
read, about prayer. Then I listed four or five things to
pray for that day.

Another thing I discovered about the Fijian preachers (in my day, not in John Hunt's day) was that they had a limited number of subjects on which they preached. And sometimes they merely changed the text and used the same sermon. So I wrote a book called *The Christian Year*. I followed all the fixtures on the Christian calendar and gave them a sermon approach for each one. I also wrote a book called *The Messiah*. The chapters in that book focused on the crisis points in the life of Jesus.

Others were also involved. We had lives of Jesus and Paul, books for children, teachers and class leaders. And, as I said above, this was not the only literary period in the history of the Fijian Church when the book publication was directed to the needs of the congregation and its leaders.

Another way the Church used printing was to produce a newspaper - a church newspaper. I was the editor of this Fijian paper for five years. It had a history that went back to the last decade of the last century, the 1890s to the 1900s. In those days, this newspaper used to publish letters from Fijian missionaries in Papua New Guinea and the Solomon Islands. So the church paper brought the field missionaries in touch with the supporters in the home church in Fiji.

So you will see that when you make a people literate and give them a Bible, before long you have to give them all kinds of aids to help in the use of the Bible and with their practical application of it in Christian living. The life of the Church is *an ongoing thing*. It goes on from generation to generation, and the Church always has to speak to each new situation in each generation. We can do this by preaching. We can also do it with literature. The Fijian Bible, when it spread out over Fiji, unified the Fijian language and made the people one. It helped to end wars between the tribes, making Fiji a happier and more unified place.

Let me finish this chapter with a story about an evangelist who carried the Gospel into the heathen interior, in the mountainous areas, in the days when there were Christian groups all around the coast of the island of Viti Levu. He lived in a little Christian village in the midst of a lot of pagan villages and had just returned from the coast where he obtained a new Bible for himself. It was two days journey down to the coast and two days journey back, and he was now home in his village for the first evening meal after his journey.

They had eaten their meal and the evangelist brought out his Bible to read. The little Christian group gathered around to hear the reading of the Bible. And just at that

moment there were war cries heard outside. The heathen were
attacking this Christian village. Everybody ran outside, and
they found that three or four of their houses were already on
fire. There were heathen with spears and clubs all around
them. The little Christian group ran to hide in the bushes.
But most of them were caught and killed. The evangelist's
wife and his little girl who were inside the house, also ran
into the bushes. The little girl grasped the Bible as she
ran. And they hid in the bushes all night. When morning came
they saw that everything was devastation. The whole village
was destroyed, and most of their number had been killed, among
them the Christian evangelist. So his wife and the little
girl, whose name was Mere, went off into the bush and started
their journey down to the coast to the Christian villages.

They found their way to a mission station, and the
heavy-hearted missionary made arrangements for the widow to go
to her own village with her daughter. There, little Mere grew
up. She went to school. She greatly treasured her Bible.
When they reached that village her mother wrote in it -

> This is Mere Nasau's book. Is it not a
> brand plucked from the burning?

Mere reached womanhood, and married. She, also, married an
evangelist. His name was Josaia Qoro.

Josaia and Mere heard about the mission to New Britain.
And God called them as missionaries to this part of German
New Guinea. They went there and served the Lord for some years.
And every morning and every evening they read from Mere's
Bible. As the years went by, Mere became ill. She died in
New Guinea and had a Christian burial there in a foreign land.

After a while Josaia returned to Fiji, and the Church
appointed him to a village in the mountains. One night he
was sitting in the house with a group of people, telling stories about the old days. There was an old man, a very old man,
who remembered the pre-Christian days. And he said, "There
used to be a village on that hill, just over there. There are
only the foundations left. But I remember as a young man, and
a heathen, raiding that village. We attacked it at night and
burned the houses, and killed the Christians. Among the Christians we killed was an evangelist." And everyone sat in silence.

Then Josaia took Mere's Bible, and he said, "Do you see
this book? This book once belonged to the evangelist you killed. It was saved by his little daughter. It was the only
thing she saved. It was taken to New Guinea, and there it was
used to preach the Gospel. And now it has come back to the
place where it began its ministry, to be used for my preaching to those who are the descendants of them who killed the

evangelist." And Josaia finished by saying, "The Word does not return void."

In my own day, one of Mere Nasau's descendants was a teacher in my school. Teaching became a lucretive profession in these later days, but this teacher gave up his position to become a theological student, and I had the pleasure of nominating him for the Christian ministry. So it goes on - and on.

Fig. 13

Joeli Bulu, Tongan Missionary to Fiji
1838 - 1877

9

The Role of the Indigenous Leader

The strength of the island churches lay in the fact that they produced their own leaders at every level. Only when converts are effectively incorporated into the church fellowship and are provided with opportunity for participation and development can this be true. In this chapter I wish to examine this process, more particularly as I researched it and experienced it in Fiji.

There was a time in Fiji when I thought I sensed a tendency for people to stress the role of the leader at the top, at the expense of the subordinate but equally important levels. I was a District Superintendent at the time and felt that many of those whom I 'supervised' were leaving decisions to me where they themselves should have taken the initiative. At the same time, I was responsible for vernacular publications, and it occurred to me that although we had a good *Life of Christ* and a *Life of Paul* in Fijian, we left the impression that Paul alone had planted the Church. I responded to the situation by writing a small book in Fijian, the title of which would be translated as *Companions of Paul*. It was about Luke, Mark, Timothy, Titus, Tychicus, Epaphroditus, Aristarchus, Aquila and Priscilla, to mention some only. Thereby I tried to give a biblical model for a factor which was really inherent in the Fijian Church system - that a church is built by subordinate leaders at all levels. Paul could have done very little without his band of splendid helpers - men of faith and courage whom he trusted and appointed to deal with all kinds of pastoral problems which emerged in the young congregations as they struggled with social and religious problems of the Graeco-Roman world. From the feed-back I received, I had reason to believe my humble effort was not in vain.

In the history of Christian mission the tendency is to
give too much coverage in reports and biography to the western missionary in charge, perhaps for promotional reasons.
But in this book I have stressed the place of the islander.
Much of the evangelism and church planting could only have
been done by the converted islanders, and the missionaries
were quite dependent on them. All people who have served as
missionaries know this truth, that many times they depend on
the skill and the goodwill of the island people with whom
they work. Indeed, I think we can go further than that and
say God wanted the islander to play a more prominent role in
the spread of the Church.

Let me tell you about a certain case in which the missionaries failed, or appear to have failed, and the island
people themselves were able to achieve the work. It concerns
a place called Somosomo. In those days this was a very wild
cannibal kingdom on the island of Taveuni, in the northern
part of Fiji. The missionaries had been in Lakeba, away down
in the south, and the people of Lau had been turning to Christianity. In doing so they had obtained a good many material
advantages because the missionaries had come to live among
them. They had acquired fish hooks, axes and hammers. The
King of this northern Kingdom, Tui Cakau, went down to visit
Lakeba which was largely Christian by this time. When he saw
all the axes, chisels, knives, fish-hooks and hammers he was
amazed. He was also angry. He said, "I am a Big Chief, and
Tui Nayau is a little chief and yet he has all this wealth of
metal axes, knives, fish-hooks and hammers, and I have none
of these things."

So he said to the Christian missionaries, "You had better come up to my island, I am a much bigger Chief than this
fellow and can do more for you." The missionaries still oc-
cupied Lakeba, but very soon after this when new missionaries
arrived from Britain, two men were sent up to Somosomo and
Tui Cakau received them. He determined that they could live
in a certain Fijian house where he could keep his eye on them.
He put the two families into one house. It only had one room.
The missionaries said they would build themselves another
house, but Tui Cakau said, "No!"

Fifteen feet away from the door was the cannibal oven,
and the missionaries had to live in that house for seven years.
They could not avoid seeing all the horrible things going on,
and every time the cannibals cooked human flesh the smell of
the ovens came to them. The Cannibal King gave the missionaries permission to preach the Gospel, but he warned his people, "If any one of you responds to that Gospel, I'll club
him and put him in the oven." So, after seven years no one,

except a few foreign carpenters, was responsive to the message which the missionaries brought.

They were very concerned about this. They said among themselves, "We believed the Lord opened the way for us to come to Somosomo. However, there are other places where the people are ready to hear the Gospel and have no preachers. The people here cannot respond even if they want to do so. Why is the Lord keeping us here as if we were in prison?" They were very discouraged. There were many times in the story of Pacific missions when the missionaries had this kind of feeling.

Somosomo was a town on the western side of Taveuni. Across the water there was a bigger island, Vanua Levu, with no missionaries at all. Then the Fijian convert who had come from Tonga with Cross and Cargill, Josua Mateinaniu, was sent to Bua in Vanua Levu. Josua found that the people there were ready to become Christian. He preached to them and in a very short time about 80 people became Christian. So here was a strange situation - the Church was not growing where the missionaries were located, but it *was* growing where there were no missionaries.

Josua Mateinaniu sent a message to John Hunt at Viwa. He said, "The Somosomo missionaries ought to be here because this is where all the opportunity is. Bua is a field ripe unto harvest but Somosomo is a green field. The harvesters ought to be in the ripe field." They talked over their failure for quite a while and prayed about it.

Then the next time the missionary ship came to visit them, after seven unsuccessful years, the missionaries decided to leave Taveuni and go to Bua. They knew that the Chief would be angry at losing his axes, fish-hooks, hammers and other tools, and so overnight, in the dark, they put their goods on the boat and sailed away. When the Chief found that the missionaries had gone he was really angry, and his people were angry with him, blaming him for their departure. Before long he was afflicted with leprosy and he died a miserable death, very much neglected by his people who said this was because he "rejected the Word of the Lord." I am not saying this was the reason, but certainly that is what the people said. And had he not done this very thing?

When the missionaries reached Bua, they began to organize the work that Josua Mateinaniu had begun, and before very long they had a large strong church in that island. Josua had laid a good foundation. There are two points to this story. The first concerns the missionaries and their time of seven fruitless years - they thought they had failed, and they had certainly suffered a great deal, but over those seven years

the four missionaries who had served in that place and lived
so closely to the people all became beautiful speakers of the
language. Each one of them was greatly used of God afterwards because he could speak the language so well. While
they were in Somosomo they did translation work and also prepared the first Fijian Hymnbook. So when anybody says that
the Somosomo missionaries were failures I suggest they look
at the story 20 years later and see what God did with those
missionaries.

But there is another point which I want to raise, namely,
what happened to these people when the Gospel was taken away?
Five or ten years later, the Gospel came back to Taveuni, and
the people accepted it. But who do you think brought it back?
Not a foreign missionary! The second time, the Gospel was
brought by the Fijian converts from Vanua Levu. So God in
his wisdom had taken away the missionaries from Taveuni to
get converts over in Bua and Nadi, and had sent these converts
to present the Gospel to the Somosomo people who would not
listen to the missionaries. And so, although the missionaries
brought the Gospel in the first place and did the translation
work, it was the island evangelists themselves who spread it
throughout the land. And that is why I am discussing the role
of the island leader and the preparation he had for his role.

Most of the stories I have told in this book have been
taken from the early years of the missions, and I have done
this because my theme is the planting of the Church in the
Pacific during the pioneering period. But as the years went
by, the character of the islands in general, and of Fiji in
particular, began to change. They became acculturated when
all kinds of new things and new values were brought in from
the outside world. As the people learned more and more new
ideas, and were educated, they became more sophisticated in a
western manner. They soon became literate. Every village had
its school and as the children were educated they acquired
more and more knowledge. Therefore it became necessary to
raise more educated leaders.

I believe that one of the strengths of the Fijian
Church has been the fact that the leaders had a little more
knowledge than the rank and file of the people. I say "a
little more" because it is dangerous if the leaders are too
far above the level of the people. In many lands the mission
of the Church has failed because people are living at a simple farming or fishing level and their pastors have high university degrees that do not relate to the occupations of the
congregation. Certainly leaders must be better trained than
the people, but just enough so to preserve their rapport and
to inspire the people to reach a higher level. This means

that it is good to find the leaders from among the people rather than from outside. A leader has to identify with the people and integrate within the social group with whom he works.

After about 50 years of church growth in Fiji, during which time the mission of the Church had been to communicate the Gospel to the unconverted tribes, this work of evangelization was almost finished. All the Fijian people could read. They had Bibles and they read them daily. They had schools and education improved. The Church at home in Fiji needed ministers who could help these better educated people. Quite obviously the situation in Fiji was changing, and clearly the kind of leaders required for one period of history were very different for those needed for another. I know of some mission societies that planned their leadership structures a hundred years ago and although the churches have been there for a hundred years they are still using the same structures. So I want to describe the development of leadership training in Fiji in a series of historical periods, and to show you, step by step, what happened in the changing patterns.

Now at the very beginning you need to visualize a missionary on a lonely mission station. There is no city or town nearby. He is alone with the island people. He has a few converts, a herald and perhaps his Bible translation informant. This is the very beginning of a new mission. And the missionary and the islander together both teach each other, each learning from the other. As time goes by more mission stations are established and more and more converts are won, so that at each mission station there would be a little congregation, and the missionary would run a school. He would have three different classes. There would be a class for men and a class for women, and a class for boys and girls. In these schools the first Fijians learned to read.

The manner in which a Fijian learnt to read is very interesting, because although the missionaries prepared the alphabet, they did not teach the people how to use it. Let us say that a man, 'A', was converted one day, and he received his alphabet. A few days later 'B' was converted and received his alphabet. His teacher is 'A'. 'A', a Christian of two or three days, teaches 'B' to read the sounds of the alphabet. The first duty given to a convert in the Christain church was to learn his letters and to teach them. And the man who knew how to put letters together in a word had to teach the man who did not yet know. And the man who could read sentences had to teach the man who could only read words. So the Christian converts taught each other to read. This was a very good scheme, because the people were excited about learning to read, and by the time they were ready to confront the missionary they could read a sentence. Then he gave them sentences with special meanings, and passages out of the Bible.

They learned not only to read and to write, but also to recite passages from the Bible. They were also trained in practical subjects. The missionaries' wives taught the women to crochet. They used to make the bodice of their underskirts entirely in crochet work. Many island women still do this. Here is a good example of cultural borrowing, where the Fijian women took a western pattern and made it indigenous. It became so indigenous that, from that day to this, the old women have passed on the art of crochet work to their daughters. And now, when the majority of missionary wives have forgotten how to crochet, the Fijians still have the skill. At one place where I was stationed we had some little doyleys that fitted the plates which were used in the communion service. They had intricate Christian symbolism worked into the design. One of these doyleys was lost, and no one had the pattern instructions, so my wife took the remaining doyley to a Fijian woman and asked her if she could copy that symbolism. The next day she brought back the two doyleys and except that the copy was newer than the original we would not have known one from the other.

So you see there was more than just the Bible that was taught in these schools. The missionaries and their wives spent many long hours teaching all kinds of crafts, and it was in this way that they got to know the language and the people.

As the work spread throughout Fiji and more and more people became Christian, the developing pattern was like this. The missionaries were scattered over the islands and each had his little school. From the school each missionary would find a few young men to go with him when he travelled through the villages preaching. Even in my time in Fiji we still made these trips (*raicakacaka*).

Very early in the mission history the need for better preachers and teachers was felt. There was an island called Viwa, the strongest church centre of them all. At the time, John Hunt was the missionary there. I narrated above how he not only translated the New Testament, but trained men to use it, preach it and interpret it. So he was in charge of the central school for the whole Group. If a missionary had two or three intelligent young men with good spiritual experiences, he would send them to Viwa. So Viwa became the first central school in the Fiji Islands, and it was adequate for the size strength and character of the Church in its day. This was called the Viwa Plan. When Hunt died, he was followed by a man named Richard Lyth. Lyth was trained both as a medical doctor and as a minister. The young men who were trained at

Viwa spread out over all Fiji and the Church began to grow in quality. People began to read the Bible, and as they grasped its message the Church "grew in grace and maturity" and so it needed better teachers still. Richard Lyth carried on this system, and he improved the curriculum.

The Church in Fiji now reached the same position as the early Church did in Acts, chapter 6. The Fijian Christians saw that there were two tasks that could come into conflict unless precautions were taken. One was the role of the evangelist and the other was the role of the teacher. The Church saw that if all were concerned with teaching there would be no evangelists, and if all were evangelists what would happen to the schools and the rising generation? So the next step was the provision of a "teacher training centre" to stand over against the "pastor/evangelist training centre". This new teacher training system was established in the 17th year of the mission and was called the Glasgow Training System.

As the years went on, another institution appeared in Fiji which was called the Big School (*Vuli Levu*). This became a school for training catechists. A catechist did the work of a pastor, but he was not ordained. And the men who were chosen for the Christian ministry were chosen from the most experienced catechists. In time, side by side with the Big School came the Theological Training Institution.

The story of the development of theological training in Fiji is a very interesting one, but a little too long to deal with here. The Church had some trouble in finding a good site for the buildings, so they tried different places, Matai Suva, Kadavu and Navuloa, and finally they came to a place called Davuilevu.

So the Church produced two things to meet the people movement intake. First, she produced a better trained type of evangelist and, second, she produced literature and Bibles at a rapid rate. So Fiji met the big conversion intake with better teaching, more Bibles, catechisms and teaching aids. In the third decade there must have been 40,000 converts in the country. How could you handle 40,000 converts in 10 years? You would need man power and literature, and the Church provided these. There were only about six or seven western missionaries in the whole Fiji Group. How could six or seven missionaries handle 40,000 converts? The island people had to do it themselves. That is why the missionaries at this stage concentrated on this kind of approach. The 40,000 converts were incorporated into the fellowship groups, and it was effectively done.

In the last chapter I used a graph which showed the converts coming in, and church buildings, sunday schools and day schools appearing. Not only was there a steady numerical increase of converts being taught the Bible, but the schools also began to spread as fast as the churches. The Church did not grow because of the schools. The schools were a fruit of the growth of the Church. I mentioned above that when they separated the teacher training as distinct from the evangelist/pastor training program, they used a method called the Glasgow System. This was a system of arranging the curriculum for *training* the children of the villages. The basic principle was training rather than teaching. The person in charge was not called a teacher but a training master. You might call him a coach.

This system of education aimed at four things, all of which we may call "training the whole person." This was based on the idea that a man has four basic characteristics. He has the *physical* side of his life which is trained by exercise. He has the *mental* side which deals with information that he receives in the brain. He has the *religious* side of his life - what he believes. Then he has the *moral* side - what he does with the things he believes, and how he lives the life he ought to live. These were the four things that were developed in the schools for the boys and girls, and it was a very good system. The children had plenty of exercise, they learned to know the difference between right and wrong, they formed good habits, and they learned the importance of prayer and religious life. So in those days the school and the church went ahead together.

On the other hand, the Big School at Davuilevu, the educational centre, trained the evangelists and catechists, and later on the best of them would become ordained as ministers. This school reflected the traditional tribal district structure of all Fiji. The people from each district would send into the school 10 or 15 of their best men. There might be 100 or 200 young men in training at one time. I ought to mention that most of the building costs were carried by the local church itself, and except for one missionary, all the regular support. No overseas money was used.

Now, let us suppose there are 10 young men from a certain island district who were at the school. It was the responsibility of the people of this district to build their dormitory, and if the roof leaked the Principal of the school would send a message to say the dormitory roof was leaking and ask if something could be done about it. Soon a canoe would come to the island with the necessary materials and the building would be repaired. You see the buildings had to be the type of construction the people themselves built. Everything had to be within the pattern, skills and knowledge of the people. They tried to make the school self-supporting. The young men would go to classes for half a day, and work in the gardens for half a day, planting and cultivating their own food. Of course, there were times of hurricane or famine, or perhaps the food just didn't grow as well as they had hoped. If they were unfortunate enough to be short of food, they would send word back to the village and the people of their own district would bring extra food to carry them through.

This Big School functioned for many years, until with the process of change it became out-of-date. Then it was replaced by a Bible School. The Bible School has two important purposes that met the situation in Fiji at the time it was planted. One of those purposes was to raise the level of candidates for the ministry, and the other was to teach young people some new directions in lay leadership. It fitted the economic changes of the country.

I think that one of the strengths of the Fijian Church is its flexibility. If conditions have changed the Fijians have recognized it and have said that as the old institution has finished its work, let it be changed and let a new institution that meets the new conditions be established. The technical school and all the different schools which have played important roles in different periods of history have come in that way.

I remember when I was in a circuit (pastorate) in Fiji, that the Fijians (who had begun to station us at that time) took me out of the pastorate and appointed me to the Theological Institution. They told me there were two things they wanted me to do. Because the life of Fiji was changing very rapidly, and there were many people migrating to the city, living a new kind of life, they needed a minister who could deal with the new set of problems; a man who was expert in English so that he could deal with all the different races. They wanted some men trained for that task. But at the same time there were still a lot of people living in the country and their way of life was very different. They feared that if a man trained for the work in the city was sent to a place in the country there might be a clash between the traditions of the people and the new ways of the young minister. This was very perceptive, and I myself had to try to pacify more than one of these congregational situations.

They also wanted some men who felt at home in the old traditional way. The Fijian Church directed me to work out a curriculum that would serve these two purposes. So for a

period of ten years we had a bi-lateral program that trained
two kinds of minister, and then we were able to go back to
a unified stream again.   This program served as a tentative
or transitional bridge from one period of history to another
while the country was going through dramatic changes.   This
is what I mean by the flexibility of the Church.

Notice that only the structures or forms had changed –
the way of doing things. We were still teaching the same
Gospel: that did not change. We were still stressing *Bible
training:* that did not change. We were still emphasizing
biblical preaching. We were still demanding a *spiritual experience* from our students. The faith was still the same,
but the forms were changing with the times.

In the individual's rise in leadership levels, let us
suppose a certain person is becoming a leader, he goes through
a series of steps. First he is a convert, then he becomes a
member on trial, then a full member. After that, in the
early days, he might have been used as an "exhorter" (that
is, a sent witness). There was another status called a "class
leader" (the leader of a group of members who met together
for prayer and testimony). Or he may have become a "prayer
leader" (which means he was officially appointed to lead
prayer meetings). If a prayer leader was called to go a step
further in leadership he would become a "local preacher", and
a local preacher might become a catechist (which meant he
supervized the work of a congregation or a group of congregations). And a catechist might feel the call to go into the
full ministry. Then he goes through another series of stages
– a theological student, a minister on probation, and in the
end he is ordained as a minister in full connexion.

In this way, at every level, there is a process of
developing leadership. With every step the emerging leader
is expected to have a fresh experience of the Spirit of God.
Here is a Church that has hundreds of catechists and local
preachers, and about 170 ordained ministers in full connexion.
When we consider the narratives of the Pacific Islands told
in this book we are not describing a mission station system
at work, we are dealing with a Church - a planted and a growing Church, autonomous and self-supporting. And when I serve
as a fellow-worker with the people in Fiji I am under their
auspices. I am a servant of the Church. My Church in Australia merely sends me to Fiji. The Fijian Church itself tells
me what they want me to do. They can appoint me to an outer
island or they can use me in the Theological Institution.
They can put me in charge of a Division or they can appoint
me as a School Chaplain.

In this chapter I have concentrated mostly on teachers, evangelists and pastors for every period of the organically developing Church. But there are many other levels of lay leadership. Earlier I mentioned Elijah Varani, the cannibal who became the peacemaker. And I have mentioned, several times, Cakabau, the cannibal King who devoured a thousand human bodies before he was converted. He was a very great man. Before he became a Christian he was a brilliant leader of his people, a perceptive administrator, by island standards, and a renowned strategist in native warfare. He was feared by all. When he became a Christian he was still a good leader, but the skills were now redirected to better goals and were used in the service of God. Not only was his personal life transformed, but he greatly helped the organizational life of the growing Church.

On the island of Bau, where Cakobau lived, there used to be a cannibal killing stone. The captives in war, who were still alive when they were brought to the island, were killed on that stone in a savage manner of which we have a surviving description. When Cakobau became a Christian he told his people that the killing stone must never again be used for that purpose. He declared he would build a church house, and he pulled down all 17 of the heathen temples that were in Bau. From the foundation stones of these temples he built a church, the walls of which are three feet thick! Then he took the killing stone on which the war victims had been killed before being cooked in the cannibal ovens, and he said, "This stone will henceforth be used to the glory of God." He turned that huge killing stone into a baptismal font, and set it in front of the congregation. "Of old," he said, "it sent people into the cannibal oven, henceforth it is going to bring them into the Kingdom of God." And when I lived on that island many years later, I baptized several people from that killing stone.

This cannibal King became a great leader and a great Christain, and when he died those who were there beside him reported his last words, "Hold me Jesus, my faith in Thee is firm!" How great a salvation that was - from a cannibal who had devoured a thousand human bodies to a Christian leader with a firm faith in the Lord. Having lived in that place, I know it well, I know people who have descended from him, and to the day I left, if there was anything I wanted to convince them of and they wouldn't listen, all I had to say was, "Your forefather Ratu Cakobau used to say..." and that was the end of it. They would say, "If Ratu Cakobau said it, its O.K."

There was a time when a party of tourists from Australia came to visit us on Bau Island, and because the tour had to be explained in English I was appointed as the tour guide. My faithful herald was beside me, but he knew very little English.   I

think he knew more than he let on! As I was talking to these
westerners about what Cakobau had done when he put the baptismal font in the church, one of them said, "What a horrible
idea, who thought of that?" My herald, who was not supposed
to know much English, turned to that tourist and said emphat-
ically, "That stone was not put there for any foreigner or
tourist. It was put there by the converted cannibal Chief
for his own people, that they should never forget the greatness of their salvation." And as I look back on the leadership patterns of the growing Church in Fiji I see something
that is very Fijian, very indigenous, and I am glad it was
that way.

A twelve-year-old boy whom Bishop Patteson took to
Norfolk Island about 1866, was Charles Sapibuana of Gaeta.
At 23 he was appointed as an evangelist to his own island.
Against much opposition he began working to win his own family, his parents, his brother, and then those of his brother's
wife. By 1878, he had a small Christian congregation on a
basis of an extended family and a few more distant affinal
relations. He ran instruction classes. The converts demonstrated their departure from the old sacrificial rituals and
the movement spread beyond the family. In 1882, when Sapibuana prepared a hundred adults for baptism he was ordained
a Church of England deacon.

The following year, the leader of opposition against
Sapibuana's work, Kalekona, and some of his people, destroyed
their charms and relics and placed themselves under instruction, and before long the baptised Christians stood at about
250. The conversion of Kalekona disturbed the pagan residue
of the island, and he himself became involved in a faith
challenge, which in turn led to a wholesale destruction of
various types of fetish (*tindalo*) and the loss of their fetish
mana, and therefore weakened public confidence in the old religion.

The movement spread all over Gaeta and required about
three years to take in all the converts and incorporate them
into the fellowship. The movement had a clear social structure expanding from a household to an extended family, affin-
ally related families, to the total social unit and beyond,
until the island had largely turned Christian.

Slightly different from the case of Charles Sapibuana
was that of another Melanesian Mission deacon, Clement Marau.

To Clement Marau, Ulawa was little more than a name.
He had met Ulawa boys at Norfolk Island, but he had no kin
connections there. In every sense of the word he was a foreign missionary. His approach to the problem of missionary
penetration is interesting. He began by witnessing to a youth

of his own age, and when he succeeded in his witness he urged the youth to present the Gospel to his own parents, and to persuade them to meet with the two youths in a gospel class. Shortly, the mother did so, and eventually the father. In time, the couple "put on the cloth" to symbolize that they had become Christian.

They stood together as a family and endured a good deal of persecution, as a result of which the neighbouring family joined their group and for a time, as a small cell of two families, they met and upheld each other in the new Faith.

At this point Marau challenged them: how would their Christian unit stand if he (Marau) were removed. As evidence of their sincerity, Marau asked them to destroy their heathen household paraphernalia, and these were formally taken to sea and thrown overboard. This was seen as a confirmation of the change of the personal religion of the two families. Now they decided to challenge the community. The occasion was a large gathering for a wedding which involved a wide network of social relationships. The Christians declared the spirits of the sacred grove no longer held them in fear, and to prove the greater power of the Spirit of God they would destroy the grove. [Marau as a foreigner could not do this.] Within the tribal pattern the matter was proclaimed as a public challenge. The Christians cut down the sacred vines, removed the fence and set the holy stone in the path to be trodden on, took their females into the sacred place, cooked and ate the sacred yams and scattered the venerated skulls and bones - every item of these in defiance of a taboo of some kind. The heathen adopted a "wait and see" attitude in expectation of dire penalties, none of which came to pass.

One by one, other small groups joined the Christians and the eight persons grew to 60 in a very short time. Eventually it became a full-scale people movement on a community level, and terminated in a power encounter at a central shrine where groups from all round Ulawa used to sacrifice, when Marau convinced Marita, the priest in charge, that Christ had a claim on him. Marita declared his intention to be baptised as a Christian and demonstrated his new faith by destroying the sacrificial shrine of his old faith.

Marau's evangelical penetration is significant. He knew that as a Merlav and not an Ulawa man he could not himself adequately deal with the Ulawa gods - the converts themselves had to demonstrate their commitment and victory. Yet he concentrated on family units and sought out the points of focus of power - taboos, sacred objects and fetishes, places of sacrifice - and he challenged his converts to demonstrate their new faith by being ready to act on it.

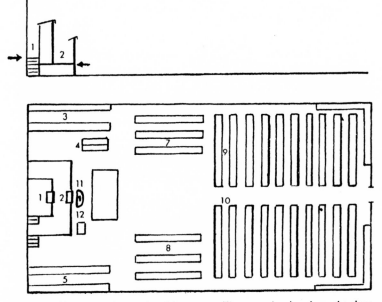

Fig. 14 –Church form and social structure. The upper drawing shows the elevation of dais and pulpit, the lower the ground plan, showing how the arrangement of furniture reflects the socioreligious relationships of the congregation. (1) Pulpit and preacher's enclosure, on the highest level, because the word is from God; (2) Reading desk and official's enclosure, from which the word of man with authority is spoken; (3) High or visiting chiefs sit here for worship; (4) Special seat and prayer stool for the chief; (5) For visiting preachers or persons with church status (resembling the old priest class); (6) Table, for presentation of offerings; (7) Choir seating; (8) Children's seating; (9) Male worshipers, according to status, those of high status in front; (10) Female worshipers, according to status, those of high status in front; (11) Baptismal font made from old killing stone; (12) "Lectern" memorial.

10

The Church Facing
Culture Change

In the last two studies on the ministry of the Word
and on the training of leaders, we studied the development of
the Church through a long *period of time*.   In the earlier
studies I was looking at the Church at a *point in time*.   In
chapter seven I gave you a term "the *continuity* of the Church."
The Church is not something that was given to us for one generation only.   It was given to our forefathers and it is
given also to us, and it will be given to our children and to
their children after them.   The Church is an ongoing institution and an ongoing program.

In the last chapter I was discussing the changes in
leadership patterns and we saw how, at different periods of
time, different kinds of leaders were needed and raised.   So
when we look at the story of the Church through time we are
considering two things.   Something which is continuous, that
goes on and on and never changes, on the one hand; and on the
other hand, something which changes with each new situation.
So the study of the Church is the study of both stability and
change.

Flexibility is important, but the key question is always *what to change* and *what not to change*.   Many people are
afraid of change.   Especially are conservative Christians
often afraid to make a change.   But change is not necessarily
a bad thing.   It is natural.   It is going on all the time.
I do not look the same today as I did 50 years ago, and if we
look at society (and that also means a church) we will always
find that in that society there are well-known mechanisms to
help people make changes.   If you belong to a group which
decides to prepare a constitution, you will find the last

clause of the constitution will read something like this:
"These rules may only be changed by two-thirds majority at
the Annual Meeting." You see, the men who wrote those rules
and regulations allowed for the fact that someday they may
want to change them.

I remember many things about the Church that my mother
taught me when I was very young. Most of those things are
now quite out-of-date, because we do not do things today as
they were done in my mother's day. It is important for us to
keep asking this question about the Church and about our mission: What needs to be changed? You know what keeps the
river pure - the fact that it flows along and never stops
still in one place. If a river dams up and does not flow it
becomes stagnant. We live in a moving, changing world, but
we need not be afraid of change, because the Lord himself
sent us out on a mission into the world, knowing that it was
a changing world.

The Bible is a book about change. Just think how long
it took for that book to be written; maybe it was 2000 years.
If we read through the Bible as a single book, the thing that
impresses us is the number of dramatic changes the people of
God passed through during their history. But God was always
with them. He knew the changes that were going on, and con-
tinually spoke to His people.

Take the day of Abraham, for example. If we go back
to the time before he was called Abraham (when he was just
Abram) we find that he came from a desert land which economically could not support many people. History tells us of two
or three huge migrations of these people up into the more fer-
tile northern lands. One of those migrations came to the city
of Ur. Abraham was tempted to remain in the city, but be mi-
grated onwards on his journey of faith. We could even say
that the story of the People of God began at that time when
Abraham went forward into the unknown in faith, and God taught
them a new way of life.

The people from whom Abraham descended used to practice human sacrifice. In the story of Abraham and Isaac and
the sacrifice on the mountain, the Lord was saying to Abraham,
"You are going to be my people, and you must not sacrifice in
the same way as your father's have done" (Gen 22:1-14). Although they still practised sacrifice, they never again sacrificed a human being, but substituted an animal. This is
what we call, in anthropology, a *functional substitute*. Sacrifice was new in form but was still a symbolic relationship
between man and God. Something continuing, and something new!

Take the day of Moses. Moses lived at the end of a period of slavery of the Children of Israel in Egypt. As slaves they were industrial brickmakers, and their way of life changed as they went out of the city into the wilderness where they became wilderness dwellers. Instead of being ruled by Pharaoh, they were led by the prophet Moses. Under a different system of political control, Moses introduced them to a different lifestyle. He gave them a new Law by which to live, and through Moses God revealed a new concept of religion. They worshipped in a tent instead of a temple. Thus, in every way the people entered a new kind of social life in the wilderness.

We could go through the Bible step by step like this. We would mention the Children of Israel as they entered into Canaan and changed from the life of wilderness into that of settled farmers in the new land. Their social structure is a Confederacy of twelve tribes and the Law lays down new marriage patterns for the new day (Num 36). Then we would go on a little further and we would pass through the rule of the Judges, said to be about 500 years. And then this structure also passed away and they were ruled under the Kingdom. The Children of Israel wanted that. God didn't want it that way, so He raised the prophets with authority to speak to the kings (I Sam 8) in the eighth, seventh, and sixth centuries when the world was passing through great upheaval among the nations. We could go on into the New Testament and discuss the changes that came because of the incarnation of our Lord. We could go into the story of the planting of the young Church. There is enough time-depth in the New Testament to see the first and second generations of the early Church. The Church is changing in the first Christian century. Look at Acts, chapters 19 and 20, and read the story of the planting of the church in Ephesus. Now read the second chapter of Revelation and you will see second generation Ephesian Christianity, which though faithful in many things had nevertheless lost its first love (Rev 2:4).

I have made this point because I believe the Bible is a book about the changing world. It has a message for people in all those different lifestyles - for the desert dwellers and the town dwellers, for the nomadic herdsmen, for the people under kings, and for people in tribal systems. There was a time when the People of God were in all these different social systems and God spoke to them. And so I am not afraid of a ministry in an ever-changing world, because I have a book which tells me of a God who speaks through all kinds of change. And I might add in passing that when I went to live with people like the Fijians, who lived close to the soil

like the Israelites I learned a lot more from them about the
Israelites in the Old Testament than I ever did in my theological training.

There are two kinds of change that will be brought
about in the story of our Christian mission. And, in a way,
the same set of rules applies in handling each of them. The
first period of change will be when the people give up their
heathenism and become Christian, and the second kind of change
is that which goes through generation after generation over
a long period of time.

I want to give you three words from an anthropologist,
the late F.E. Williams. He was what we call an applied anthropologist. Applied anthropology means that the theories
you learn in anthropology are applied to situations in life.
(1) The first criterion he used for discovering *what* ought
to be changed and *how* it ought to be changed is *Maintenance*.
He was asking the question, what elements in this society
must we maintain? What are the things we see that are good
and ought to be preserved? He was saying you never change
anything until you understand its function, and if it is effective. (2) The second word he used is *Expurgation*. It
means – What should be discarded? Presumably it is either
bad or it has ceased to serve its true function. It is out-
of-date. (3) Finally, he had another word, *Expansion*. How
may this way of life be expanded? What new things can be in-
novated or put into it?

So F.E. Williams was saying, "Before you do away with
the pagan system or a heathen idea, or anything cultural in
the ways of the people to whom you go, you ask three questions: What do these people have that is worth saving? What
do they have that ought to be thrown away? And what new
things can be brought and added to their way of life to make
it better?" These are three good questions. Not all missionaries have asked these questions or listened to the answers.

Let me tell you about two island churches which I know.
These are very similar people. They are both Melanesian.
They have the same style of life in many things, but their
churches are very different. Remember the three questions as
I tell you how these churches differ –

> First Case: It is Sunday morning and we hear the beat-
> ing of a drum. It is a wooden drum, cut by an island
> people, the old kind of drum they have used as far back
> as they can remember. There is a special rhythm that
> is being beaten. There was a day when that rhythm call-
> ed people to war, but now it calls them to church. I
> go into the church building and find the people doing

things in their own way. The service is held in the
language of the people. All the minor duties that have
to be done are done by the lay people of the island
themselves. There is an island preacher, the choir is
entirely comprised of island leaders. They sing their
own kind of music. The people chant the catechism in
their own language. It is led by islanders. The
notices are given by islanders, and islanders take up
the collection. In every way it is an island service.

Second Case: In another place, I go into a church of
the same demonination. A European opens the church and
keeps the keys. There is a choir, but they sing foreign
hymns in English. The choir master is a foreigner. The
preacher is an Englishman and the sermon is in English.

Consider these two churches for a moment. They are
the same denomination in the same part of the world. In the
first case, before discarding anything that was wrong, the
missionaries had asked what are the good things they could
keep. Of course they had kept the language, and they had
kept the music. The missionary in the other case had said,
"All these things are bad. They are tied up with heathenism
and the people will be heathens as long as they do them so
let us get rid of them all," and he had made it a thoroughly
foreign church.

In the first case there was maintenance, and in the
second there was not. True, of course, there will be many
things that have to go when a people becomes Christian -
cannibalism, infanticide and widow strangling had to go in
Fiji. Our Lord came to this earth to bring about change, and
it is right that we should consider those things that have
to be discarded. However, quite often those things that are
bad or obsolete and therefore have to go, have served a good
function in the heathen past. It may be that we have to find
some Christian functional substitute to take the place of the
old thing that was not ethically Christian.

The ceremonial buildings that the Solomon Island people used to make engaged their craft skills. Their war canoes were made of wood that was died black in the swamps and
skillfully inlaid with mother-of-pearl. Their buildings were
decorated with very fine designs woven with dyed twine. What
happens to the arts when a people becomes Christian? There
are two ways of looking at this. You may either say the dying of the wood, the making of the canoes, the inlaying of
the mother-of-pearl, and the making of the twine are all associated with heathen rites and usages, so we will throw it
all away. Or you may say that it is a good skill; it is a

beautiful string that is made; it is a fine piece of woodwork;
it is beautiful inlaying and it is a skill that is worth pre-
serving. The skill can be used either for good or for bad.
You may use it for building a war or headhunting canoe, or
you may use it for making furniture and beautifying a church
building.

The Church of England people in the Eastern Solomons
have preserved all these arts, but instead of using them for
the old heathen practices, they have used them for Christian
purposes. And it is very important that we should find such
functional substitutes, so that people can retain their skills,
their craftwork, their music, their language and their art.

A people may become very poor, economically poor, by
becoming Christian if they loose an art or a skill. The people of Malaita in the Solomon Islands used to have an industry
which we will call "porpoise fishing". A porpoise is a huge
sea creature like a fish. Its teeth are small, but there are
hundreds of them. The people used to go out and fish for the
porpoise and get the teeth, clean them and make them into
necklaces, which were the bride-wealth with which they got
their wives. So this was a means of revenue to them, and some
of them were very rich because of the things they made with
porpoise teeth. And then a large social unit of the people
became Christian, but the evangelist who guided them in their
new way of life forgot the importance of maintenance. He said
that porpoise fishing was wrong because it was done with heathen rites. You prayed to the spirits of the sea before going to catch the fish. Subsequently a new island pastor came
to minister to them.

He asked the Christians, "How come you are so poor and
that a heathen is so rich?

And they said, "Because they are heathen and they get
the porpoise teeth which makes them rich. That is a heathen
thing and we don't do it."

And the pastor said to them, "This is a crazy thing.
Who made the sea? Who created the porpoise? Who put the porpoise out there? God did that. It is his sea, and they are
His fish, and you have as much right to that trade as the
heathen have. Perhaps more, because you know the Creator,
and they don't."

And then they asked, "What, then, will we do?"
He said, "We'll all go porpoise fishing."
"But the heathen will be angry," they said.
"Never mind that, they don't own the sea. In any case
we will go with prayer. We will all gather together with our
canoes and our fishing gear and we will go down to the beach,
and there we will pray to the Lord of Heaven, that He will
give us a good harvest of porpoise."

And the heathen were very angry. And they said, "You can't do this. This is a heathen not a Christian practice. If you pray to your God on the beach you will chase all the porpoises out of the sea."

But the pastor was determined and he brought all the Christian people down to the beach with their things ready and they prayed to the Lord, that he would give them a harvest, and that this industry would be available for the Christain people. And they got their canoes and went out to fish.

And the heathen came down to the shore. They walked backwards and forwards and they lamented, "We'll lose all our fish."

And the Christians fished all that day and never caught a fish. They came home that night and the heathens said, "We told you so!" They prayed again the next morning and went out the next day. Again - no fish! And they went out the third day. Still no fish! And the fourth and the fifth and the sixth! But, remember the story of Jericho!

On the seventh day they went out, and they got the biggest catch of porpoise that they ever remembered in the history of that island. I lived for six weeks on that island, in a leaf house with the people, and I know that porpoise fishing is now a Christian industry, and the Christians are no longer the poor people. The Lord has blessed them.

The point I want to make, of course, is that porpoise fishing was not a heathen custom. It was heathen only because they performed heathen religious rites with it. And if the first evangelist had said, "Let us save the fishing, and let us substitute a Christian prayer rite for the heathen rite," he would have saved a lot of trouble. This is a functional substitute. The people had a felt need, an economic need. They still had that economic need after they became Christain and they needed to satisfy it in some way or other.

I have given you some examples of art and craft skills that may be preserved and made Christian, and now I have added an economic example. This may be applied also to social organization. We narrated earlier about a cannibal who built a church. Let me give you the ground plan and elevation of the church that he built (Fig.13). Notice the positions of the pulpit, the lectern, the seats, the communion table and the killing stone. Although there are innovations (cultural borrowing) from western worship, the building reflects the social structure and was not designed by a missionary. The plan was the work of the converted cannibal chief, and his people built it from the temples he destroyed. It shows all the important things about Fijian social relationship. The

men sit on one side, and the women sit on the other. Now, if
I was a stranger and I walked in and sat down in the wrong
place, the church steward would come to me and say," Please
Sir, your seat is over there." He knew it would mean someone
would be uncomfortable if I was sitting, say, among the women.
According to my status I would sit in the seat called "the
place of the work." If any missionary, Fijian minister or
catechist who is employed in the work of the Church is visiting this church, he sits there. That is his place, and he
doesn't sit anywhere else. If there are any visiting chiefs
who are important, they sit in the place of the chiefs. What
the people are saying by that is this. "We are honoring you.
You do not belong in one of our groups so we have given you
a place of your own so we will know who you are." There is
also a status series going back through the congregation, the
people with the higher status being in the front.

The plan shows a reading desk. If anybody wants to
make an announcement - the collection, say, or the meetings
that are going to be held during the week, or if the leading
layman wants to tell people about a work program, the official
will come and stand at the reading desk to make the announcement. The height of this platform is a little above the floor;
but note there are steps leading up to the pulpit. This is
the place where the Word is preached. The idea is that it
does not matter who the chief is, if he is just making an
announcement about the meetings or a special collection he
comes to the platform but no further. But if he is preaching
the Word of God, whether he is a chief or a commoner, whether
he has status ot not, he goes right up to the highest place -
the pulpit.

There are some old things that are maintained here, as
Williams suggested. The pattern of relationships between the
men and women is still preserved. The idea of welcoming a
visitor and finding the respectful place for him is preserved.
The idea of making announcements is preserved, but the idea of
preaching the Word of God is new, and it is given the highest
place. This is what Williams called "expansion". The sacred
place of the old religion has been discarded. The preaching
of the Word took the place of the cannibal rites. It is a
functional substitute. The baptismal stone is in itself a
functional substitute, the stone is still there so the people
will always remember, but it is there for *a new purpose* altogether.

Let me now tell you something about how the Fijians
take up the collection. The idea of a collection was not
really a foreign idea. It was only in the passing of the
years that it become a "money thing". I have already described the original collections, how they were made in fans

and mats and pots and all kinds of things. The people had no
money, but their wealth was in the form of goods. I have been
in a village when a presentation of goods has been made to a
party of people visiting for a church meeting, and I have seen
the people bring forward their goods in a long line, one behind the other. In a very big gathering you may see right to
the end of the village, and stretching out beyond, a long line
of people coming in, one with a mat, one with a basket of
food, one with a pot, others with fans, and so on. They will
stack the things up in a big heap on the village "green",
and if there are not many people in the village when they present their gift they will sneak around the back of the assembly and come through the line again, with another gift. This
will go on for a long time until all the gifts are stacked up
in front of the leaders of the meeting.

I remember one conference like this when the people
who were giving the gifts were salt-makers. They used to go
out into the saltiest part of the swamp and collect the salt,
dry it and put it into baskets shaped like pots that stood
about a foot or so high. There must have been 300 of them
presented that day. The point was, the people had no money,
but whatever wealth they had they gave to the Lord. Origin-
ally this was done for the heathen temples in this way, so
when heathenism passed, Christianity maintained that custom.
So the old form became new with Christian meaning, and they
still use this method quite often for taking up their church
offerings, which are now mostly money gifts. Even if it is
in a small church building they will still use this system and
everyone will come up and put his collection on the table. If
it happens to be the annual collection then this is a very
big function and the people will divide into their social
groups, and their family subdivisions. And each family will
give a musical item and take its offering. At the annual
offering it may be that on that one night the gifts will carry
the finances of the church for the whole year. I have heard
critical European visitors say, "How much show it is!" But
that is not true, because they are doing it in their own way,
and they love it, and they get a lot of excitement out of it.
I'm sure they would say the Lord loves a cheerful giver.

Now I think that sometimes there are also cultural values that may be preserved. Let me go back to the church on
the island of Bau. I have told you elsewhere that I lived
with my family for three years on that little island. We were
the only white people living there. I was not the pastor of
the church. I was the District Supervisor, but the island
pastor lived there also. While we were there the church building had fallen into disrepair. There had been two hurricanes
and an earthquake, the roof was in a bad way, and the walls,

although they were three feet thick, were nevertheless cracked.
Much of the woodwork in the church had been eaten by insects
and it needed repair. It was really a big job and the responsibility of the people who were there. It was not my job,
but I was very much embarrassed because of the way it looked,
and because I was the District Superintendent I had a right to
speak about it. I could not do anything but speak.

One day I asked one of the leading elders, "Are you in-
tending to repair this church?"

And he told me, "The Government Chief in the village
has all the money ready to repair it, but he's holding up the
Lord's work because of an argument about who is to do the re-
pairing job. It is a very big job, and it means the spending
of a lot of money."

In this village there were three or four young men who
were trained carpenters, and commuted to work in the city
every day. They said, "We are carpenters. We live on this
island. We should get the job and earn the money." But the
Chief said their work would not be good enough, and so they
argued about it.

So I said to the elder, "Next year, you are having a
very big function here and people will be coming from all over
Fiji. Do you want them to see the building as it is?"

And he stated the problem for the second time, so I
asked, "Why don't you do it in the old chiefly way?"

His eyes lit up and he said quickly, "Is that O.K. by
you?" I answered, "Sure it is!" So he immediately went to
the Chiefs in the village and told them my mind on the matter.

They followed the old pre-Christian pattern for building a temple. They got together a presentation of gifts and
a whale's tooth (which is the instrument with which you can
make a request) and they sent the herald with these presenta-
tions to the people of the village of Daku, asking, "Will you
restore the church at Bau." And the Daku people were so
pleased at being asked to do this that they said, "Yes, certainly we will."

Now, this meant that they would do the work without pay.
However, on the other hand, they could go to the chief and ask
for any building materials they wanted. They could ask for
the best wood, and they could reject anything that was cracked
or knotted. They could ask for as much as they wanted, but
they had to finish the job without pay. In the old pre-Christian times, the Daku people were known as the people who kept
all the heathen temples in order, and so here you have a functional substitute. Their program was being applied to the
Christian church, and when the men were ready to do the work
one of their heralds came to my house and asked politely,

"We want you to come and pray with us as we start work. To us this is a religious rite, we are about to restore the temple of God. We want you to pray for us, and our tools, and the work." They had cleared the building and everything was ready. Work tools were all together, and the workmen were standing in a ring around them. I went down to the village to pray with them as they began to restore the house of God.

Just before I began the prayer, the head of the party said, " I want you to know that to all of us workmen, this is a sacred task. Every man in this team is a dedicated Christian. I have not allowed any smoker or drinker to be in this team. Our hands are clean and we do not want to dirty them in any way, for this is God's house. Will you now pray for us and our work." And I prayed for them, there and then, with some enthusiasm, and the work they did was really superb.

They stayed there for some months. They asked the Chief for new materials and beautiful timber. The Chiefs had to supply their meals. But they left the building in a state that was really beautiful to behold.

This is a little story about how certain aspects of culture were maintained, and a new gospel was brought in, and by it their finer values were sanctified and deepened because they had become Christian. In their own way the people were facing change with these three criteria - what to maintain, what to discard, what to expand!

Fig. 15

Ratu Cakobau, The Converted Cannibal

11

The Indigenous Record of the Expanding Church

Throughout this book I have compared the experiences of the New Testament Church with those of the indigenous church-planting evangelists of the South Pacific. I have tried to bring focus on some of the basic elements of a biblical theology of mission - the sovereignty of God, the missionary call, the missionary thrust, the persecution to be endured, conversion and commitment, the emergence of the Church, the ministry of the Word, the training of leaders and the confrontation with the changing world.

In this chapter I wish to draw these elements together informally, and chat about one or two points that arise from their interaction.

One of the really interesting discoveries when you read the New Testament *as a book*, is that you see how the Christian Church spread from Jerusalem and Antioch to all parts of the Roman world. Not only did the movement plant congregations but it also created its own literature. It wrote its own history. We ought to stress more the great importance of writing up the story of the Lord's work. The writings in the New Testament (like the four Gospels) are records of events in the life of our Lord. The Acts of the Apostles is the record of the spread and growth of the Church. But there are other books in the New Testament, letters which were written to churches, and others to individuals. These records and letters are "the very stuff of history". Almost everything we know about the Church of the first century is found in these writings.

They are important because they place into the pages of history first, the message of God's salvation for mankind as demonstrated in the incarnation, death and resurrection of our Lord; second, the Lord's commission to his followers to communicate that message to all peoples; and third, the narrative of the obedience of his followers to this commission and the emergence of the Church in the process. It was this missionary Church which produced these written records, now described as the New Testament.

Something very similar happened in the South Pacific with the diffusion of the Gospel and the planting of churches. The Pacific Church created its own historical record. There are reports, diaries and letters that tell us how the Church grew and what the faith of the early Christians was like. And the theology and the historical narratives that I have been giving you in this book have come from those records. So the main point I want to make in this chapter is that this valuable historical record of the workings of God in the South Pacific has inspired me and helped me. I know how the Church grew, and I know what stopped its growth. I know the triumphs of its faith, its problems and persecutions, because the early Christians wrote up the story in their letters and reports, and I have read them.

This has happened in many mission fields, but often, as the years go by, many of the records get lost, and with the loss of the records, diaries and letters this story of the men of faith who built the Church perishes with them. Because of these lost records many young Churches do not know their history, and have forgotten the great things God has done in bringing their Church into existence. One of the purposes of *missiology*, or better *missiography*, is to recapture the secrets of those early written records so that this present generation does not forget the greatness of its salvation.

I would also hope that the present day island pastors and missionaries would learn to keep a written record of their travelling the road with Christ; because in very truth they are engaged in the process of writing contemporary church history.

In the course of my study of the missionary documents of the South Pacific, and particularly of those of Fiji, I have found those of the British and Australian missionaries rich in information; but by far the most exciting are those written by the South Pacific Islanders themselves.

Few things are as exciting to me as to discover some old letter written by a Fijian a hundred years ago, either printed in some missionary paper or in his own handwriting.

I have at home a collection of 42 letters written in the Fijian language in the 1890s. They were written by the first Fijian missionaries to Papua (what was then "British New Guinea") and these letters from the Papuan islands tell of the struggles the Christian evangelists had trying to give the Gospel to the people of Papua who were still cannibals. They are very exciting letters to read, but do you see what we really have in these documents? Here were Fijians who had gone to New Guinea, who were planting the Church there and were unconsciously creating their own written record. They have recorded all sorts of facts about how the Church was planted, and how people battled with paganism. The story would have been completely lost if they had not written these letters.

I have two small notebooks at home about half an inch thick, one of these was written by Joeli Bulu and the other by Jemesa Havea. These men were Tongan missionaries to Fiji. They both gave their lives to Fiji and lived there until they were old men, and died there. Their notebooks are written in Fijian, not in Tongan. Here are exciting stories of the planting of the Church, and the strong faith of the young Christians. Of these two autobiographies, Jemesa Havea's has never been translated, it is still only found as a handwritten document in Fijian. The missionary, Lorimer Fison, translated Joeli Bulu's life story, and I have a copy of it in English as well as the Fijian. I value this little book very highly. For the last thirty years I have not seen one come up for sale and I would not part with mine for a month's wages.

From Melanesia comes another one, the story of Clement Marau, a Merlav (Banks Islands) boy, Church of England convert on Norfolk Island, who went as a missionary to Ulawa in another part of the Solomons which was then completely pagan. When Marau left Ulawa there was a strong Church there. He wrote the story in the Mota language and the missionary anthropologist, R.H. Codrington, translated it into English eighty years ago. It is a fascinating story of church planting from an islander's point of view.

Shortly before World War II another similar book appeared. It was the autobiography of Osea Ligeremaluoga, translated by a missionary, Ella Collins. This comes from New Ireland, one of the northern islands of what was German New Guinea. The book tells the story of this young fellow who was born a pagan, and how he grew up and became a Christian and then a missionary teacher, and a preacher. In the early part of the book he talks about the customs of his tribe, about how New Ireland boys were initiated as men. He tells of many customs that sprang from a pagan value system - how a child would be buried with his father when the father

died, for example. He describes burial customs at length.
He tells how the magicman made rain, and how they practised
sorcery. He tells about how they were troubled by different
kinds of spirits. Indeed, the book has a whole chapter on
their tribal beliefs about spirits. And then the last few
pages of his book are about his life as a Christian preacher.
He tells about how he first came to be a preacher, and how he
preached his first sermon. I think this was perhaps the finest sermon in the collection (he gives the full outline of
several of his sermons), a sermon on "God is a Spirit". If
you put his pre-Christian belief of the spirits of the tribe
over against his Christian sermon on God, you see a whole
world of difference in the life and experience of this young
man after conversion.

And I have another little book like this about a man
called Sefanaia Bilivucu. He was a Fijian herald, and therefore a layman. He gives a Christian layman's view of the
planting and growth of the Church. His story was put together
for printing by Fison. So there must be a great body of books
like this, or letters, or handwritten manuscripts, scattered
about the world in the archival and manuscript collections. I
mean material written by the South Pacific islanders themselves. From Tonga, Samoa and Fiji (the South Central Pacific)
through Melanesia into Papua and New Guinea converts became
literate, and missionary anthropologists like Lorimer Fison,
R.H. Codrington and George Brown encouraged them to write down
their experiences.

Then there is another kind of biography in which some
missionary very much indebted to and inspired by the faith
and ministry of some South Pacific Islander has written his
life story. These are stories *about* island Christians rather
than stories *by* island Christians. Although they are narrated
through missionary eyes, even so they are crammed with important historical facts. I mean, books like Nicholson's *The Son
of a Savage* (the story of Daniel Bula of Vella Lavella): Hop-
kins' *From Heathen Boy to Christian Priest* (Jack Taloifuila
of Malaita); and Rycroft's *From Savagery to Christ* (David Vule,
also from the Solomons). Together with these published books
we may search out in the missionary archives hundreds of short
biographical accounts of South Pacific Island evangelists.
The men who have written these accounts have all known their
subjects personally as they have also known the islands where
they worked and the people whom they sought to win for Christ
- so these books are far more than just library research.

Perhaps I have written enough to establish the truth
of my claim that a great deal of information does exist in
out-of-the-way places for reconstructing the story of church

planting in the South Pacific from the point of view of the
island evangelists and pastors, and to express the hope that
someday what I have tried to do in a popular way in this book
will be researched, documented and published by some South
Sea Islander. If I may return to my New Testament model, I
should remind the reader again that when an evangelistic thrust
(as we see recorded in the Book of Acts) penetrates into the
world with a program of church planting it is actually creating its own history - be it oral or written. In the islands,
the spread of the Gospel made the people literate. The translation of Scripture brought with it printed catechisms, hymn
books, preaching and teaching aids, the artifacts of the new
community and the new skills of reading and writing. If we
examine these artifacts we can reconstruct the picture of
what the church was, what it believed, how it was organized
and how it grew, in just the same way as we do with the Early
Church when we read the New Testament and the literary artifacts of the 1st and 2nd Centuries.

Now, for the remainder of this chapter, I want to take
some of these vernacular literary artifacts and examine their
contents. Quite apart from the value of the books in putting
together the whole story, there is another value. These books
are the story of God at work in human life.   Sometimes we
read theology books and forget that the important thing is not
just the theology, but the theology as you see it working in
the daily life of people. You may read 20 books, say, on
salvation, or reconciliation, but what is the value of it if
salvation and reconciliation are not manifest in the life of
the community to which you minister. And what I have been
trying to say in this book is that the important theology of
the Christian faith has to be lived out in the lives of people.
These little autobiographical books are records of conversions.
They tell the story of converts who suffered and lived through
persecution, and yet remained true to the faith. They show
how Christians bore witness in all sorts of places. They show
how Christians gathered together and formed into Churches.
But above all, they are stories of faith - faith that was
rooted in the Bible, faith that was not just knowledge, not
just the thing known to be true, but faith that people were
ready to act on.

Let me illustrate one or two important points from
some of these books. I mentioned a little book of Jemesa Havea's that I had. Jemesa was out sailing in a canoe with several others from the village. They were headed for the island of Beqa when a storm came upon them, a real hurricane.
A Fijian canoe has a very big sail, and if the wind is too
strong it can tip the canoe over. (There is a special tech-

nique of crew behaviour for shifting the weight on the canoe
in order to keep it sailing.) In this particular storm they
were so much in danger of the canoe tipping over that they
pulled the sail down and ran before the wind. Jemesa was the
only Christian on the canoe, but he was a brave man of faith.
The storm was so bad that everyone expected the canoe to be
capsized and they were all afraid - all except Jemesa, because
he knew that the Lord ruled the storms. A heathen asked him,
"Jemesa, are you not afraid that we will all be drowned?"

     And Jemesa answered (I am giving you his actual words
which I copied out of his notebook), "Nothing is difficult for
God. There are many islands in these waters. If it is God's
will for us to live he will bring us to land somewhere."

     Then he looked at the heathen and added, "But if it is
the will of God to take us to another place beyond the storms
we ought to consider whether or not our canoe is headed for the
right place."

     He then turned to the other heathens and paused for
his words to take effect, "Is your canoe heading for destruction or eternal life?"

     They were all sailors and there were no more questions.
And there were many sharks following the canoe! For two days
and two nights they drifted without the sail, where, they did
not know. On the third day they came to the island of Nairai
and the canoe drove hard on the sand.

     Now the island of Nairai had only just become Chris-
tian. I have already told you what their belief had been when
a canoe came ashore like that. The people who escaped death
at sea would be put in the cannibal oven, because they were
regarded as a gift of the gods. But the newly Christianized
Nairai people welcomed the strangers from the canoe, brought
them in to the fire, warmed them and gave them food. And the
heathens from the canoe were amazed that their lives had been
spared. They were 30 degrees off their course, and they were
120 miles away from the island to which they had been sailing.
And because they were so amazed at having been spared, the
heathen said to Jemesa Havea, "Tell us more of this life eternal you questioned us about on the ship in the storm." This is
the type of witness that these men gave fearlessly in extreme
danger.

     The autobiography of Joeli Bulu begins with the story
of his conversion. He tells of when he was a heathen and he
heard a preacher in Tonga speak about "the beautiful land."
This was a sermon on heaven, and the preacher was contrasting
the Christian idea of heaven with the Tongan notion of an
afterlife. Joeli's great desire now was to obtain assurance
that he would go to this happy land. But when his family

heard this they were very angry. They had a family meeting, and the heathen priest became inspired [that is, the heathen family spirit had possessed him]. The spirit in the priest shook him so that his whole body trembled, and he shouted out aloud, "Why has he forsaken me? I have kept him. I have preserved him since he was a little boy. Now he wants to leave me!" And as the spirit had spoken so angrily in this way, the family said, "We will punish him! We will club him! He shall die today!" Whereupon Joeli cleared out into the bush, and there he prayed. The early part of Joeli's life was a struggle between "a desire to join the life of the Church" and "his fear of the anger of his family."

And then he goes on to tell how he passed beyond an awareness of the Christian hope to a real spiritual experience. He was listening to an address by a missionary who was standing under a tree on the village green. He was preaching on "the wheat and the tares", and Joeli tells how, as he thought about "the good seed and the bad seed growing together," the Lord said, "Joeli, you think you have been among the wheat, but you are among the tares. You think you have been good seed, but you are bad seed." And at this time he began to discover the meaning of repentance. For a moment he forgot the beautiful land which was his first motivation. So he goes on from step to step in the faith. As the missionary shared his own experience of repentance and faith, Joeli thought,

We are like two canoes, sailing bow to bow, neither one faster than the other, both going together. [This was when he was speaking of his repentance.] But he went on to speak of his faith in Christ, the forgiveness of sin, and the peace and joy which he found in believing. And then I said to myself, 'My mast is broken, my sail is blown away, and his canoe has gone clean out of sight and I am left drifting helpless over the waves.' [And then Joeli goes on to tell how he came into that experience himself as well.] I saw the way and I, even I, also believed and lived. I was like a man fleeing for his life from an enemy behind him, groping along the wall of a house in the dark to find a door, and lo, a door is suddenly opened in my face, and straightway I bounded in and was free. Thus it was with me as I listened to the words of the missionary.

This is the way Joeli Bulu starts his story, by telling how he came to faith in Christ, and the book is full of wonderful incidents of the life of faith that this man lived. It was out of this little book that I got the story of the Christians sitting in the village when the heathen came in upon them and surrounded them. I would like to include with

these stories of witness bearing, conversion and persecution
some experiences of faith itself. Observe the theological
point in the two stories that I am about to share with you.
*There is a difference in believing a thing to be true and
having faith enough to act on it.* I know that when I want
light I can push a little button and the light will come, I
know that is true. I believe that. But I will never get the
light till I push the button.

I need the faith to act in the expectation of what I
know all the time. In my early life I lived in a Christian
home and was taught the Bible. I went to Sunday School.
I knew the Bible fairly well. If anyone had said to me, "Do
you believe in the truth of the Bible and that Jesus is or
Saviour?" I would have said, "Yes, I believe it." Yet I can
well remember to this day, the time a man [I don't know who
he was] challenged me on the point of whether I was really
ready to act on that thing I knew to be true. I remember
clearly taking that step of faith. So there is a difference
in believing a thing as a fact and being prepared to put your
life on it and do it. I think of all the island evangelists
whose stories I've read, and the man who best illustrates
this point was Bilivucu. He was a herald and he took the
name Sefania when he became a Christian. Let me tell you one
of Bilivucu's experiences.

Bilivucu tells about a man who was angry with him and
hit him on the head with a cooking pot. The man was angry
because he was a heathen and Bilivicu was witnessing and trying to convert him to Christianity. Bilivucu was zealous
about this and kept at it for so long, that the man lost pat-
ience, took up a cooking pot and hit Bilivucu on the head.
And Bilivucu went back to his house with a very bad headache.
He asked himself what he should do. "I try to tell this man
the good news," he said, "and all he does is hit me on the
head with a pot. But my heart is more sore than my head."
One reason why Bilivucu was sore was because a man never hits
another *man* with a cooking pot. A cooking pot is a thing of
the kitchen. This is to treat him like a woman. You hit a
man with a war club. He wouldn't have worried if he had been
hit with a club, but to be hit with a cooking pot, and to be
treated like a woman, that didn't appeal to Bilivucu the herald at all. It showed his message was despised.

While sitting there in his house, Bilivucu looked up
and saw his old pre-Christian warclub hanging on the wall.
When he had become a Christian he had taken his warclub and
had hung it on the wall saying, "That will remind me of what
I was before I became a Christian." And Bilivucu was torn
between two thoughts. "He hit me with a cooking pot, I should

hit him with that club," and "No, I'm a Christian, I should
not retaliate." Then he put up his hand to take the club.
Then he said, "No! No!"

In the end he saw his open Bible on the floor beneath
the club. He had been reading it earlier at his morning
prayers. He took it in his hands saying, "Maybe the Lord will
tell me what I ought to do." Almost immediately his eyes fell
upon the words, "Blessed are they which are persectued for
righteousness sake, for theirs is the Kingdom of God." His
anger left him, and he tells us his soul was filled with joy.
He went out into his own kitchen and got the best cooking pot
he could find and returned to the house of the man who had
hit him on the head. At the door, as the Fijian custom is,
he gave a call to say he was coming in. When the heathen man
heard the voice of Bilivucu he looked around quickly and grab-
bed his club. But Bilivucu entered with the new cooking pot
and said to the angry man, "I'm sorry you broke your pot on my
head. Here is a new one." The man was amazed, and when he
was able to speak, he said, "This is a wonderful thing.   I
break a 'thing of the kitchen' on your head and you give me a
new one in its place." And there and then he made an atonement in the ceremonial way, and asked for more information
about this power that had changed Bilivucu's life.

Then he asked Bilivucu, "Why did you do this when I
treated you the way I did?" And Bilivucu pointed him to the
Book. "The Word of the Lord says, he who is persecuted for
righteousness sake shall have the Kingdom of God, and because
you persecuted me I may claim the promises of the Kingdom of
God. So it does not injure my Christian life to be treated
like this." The man said, "That is a wonderful Word, tell me
more about it." So Bilivucu was able to witness to the man
who had now a hearing ear as he never had before.

Let me tell you one more thing about Bilivucu, the
herald of Kabara to chiefly Lakeba (*Mata ki Lakeba*). There
was, in his day, a white man's ship which brought a disease
to his island. It soon became an epidemic and a number of
people died. Among the afflicted there was a kinsman of Bilivucu who was very ill indeed, and everyone knew he was dying.
He was so close to death that his relatives began digging the
grave. Bilivucu was in his own house reading the Bible and
meditating on the book of James.

There is a passage in James which reads, "Is there any
sick among you, let him call the elders of the Church, and let
them pray over him, anointing him with oil, in the name of the
Lord, and the prayer of faith shall save the sick, and the
Lord will raise him up."

Bilivucu read that passage, then suddenly he jumped
up and took his Bible and a bottle of oil and ran to his heathen kinsman's house. There he found him lying close to the
fire and "his face was the face of the dead." "I am come to
report a great thing to you," Bilivucu said to him. "You have
been offering that fat pig of yours to your gods, and many
other gifts as well, in order that you might live. But your
sickness has grown worse and worse, and here this God of mine
will heal you for nothing if I ask him."

Bilivucu then read the passage of Scripture, and he
said to the man, as a Fijian herald would, "Will I report the
state of your health to my God?" And the sick man sighed,
"Yes, that I may live." So Bilivucu poured the oil on him
and rubbed it all over his body and he knelt down and prayed
to the Lord and [I give you his own words]

...before I came to the end of my prayer, he threw off
his covering and sat up. 'I live!' he cried. His wife
was sitting beside him, and he said to her, 'Bring hith-
er a sulu, that I may put it on. Put one on yourself,
and let all our children have one apiece. This house is
Christian today.'

[The putting on of the garment was the sign of becoming Christian.] Everybody was excited and delighted because this heathen man through his sickness and healing had become a Christian. He put himself under Bilivucu to be taught the Bible
properly. And everybody was pleased, "except the young men
who had dug the grave for nothing and had to fill it in" as
Bilivucu reported it. Here was a man who read the Word of
God, believed it, and was ready to act upon it.

In the narrative of the planting of the Church in the
South Pacific there is no end to experiences of this kind -
stories of conversion, of witness bearing, of faithful men
enduring persecution, of the planting of the Church. But
above all, they are stories of faith, faith that was rooted
in the Bible, and faith that showed men who were ready to act
on what the Bible told them to do, and it takes this kind
of faith to plant a Church.

Epilogue:
The Anchorage

One of the great missionaries of the cannibal days in Fiji was Lorimer Fison. He died in Melbourne, in 1907. I had heard that his youngest daughter, now very old, lived somewhere in a Melbourne suburb, and I determined to visit her. All I knew was the name of the street and that she lived in an old-fashioned house somewhat back from the pavement. I found the street, a long one, and walked along looking for some indicator. Eventually I found myself confronting a name on a gate, *"Nai Kelekele"*. Surely this was it. Not only was the word Fijian, but it declared the place to be "The Anchorage". Who but a man who had sailed the island waters in a deep-sea canoe would choose a name like that?

For three years I lived on the chiefly island of Bau. One of the interesting archaeological features of this island is the system of canoe docks built into its very foundations to this day. The craft which anchor there now are small. But there was a time when Bau was a busy metropolis of 3000 people, mostly engaged in the business of war.

We have the description of the arrival of a new war canoe, the *Ra Marama*, a vessel 118 feet in length, which was to be a gift to Ratu Cakobau, the Chief of Bau. It had taken a whole village a year to build, accompanied with a wide range of religiosocial ceremonial. But the effect of the Gospel was beginning to take effect, and the Chief of Somosomo had neglected some of the cannibal rites and sacrifices associated with its launching. The vessel sailed to Bau and came into the port. As the sailors let down the mast, its foot slipped from its socket and a sailor was killed. Cakobau immediately asked if the launching sacrifices had been neglected. He demanded the cannibal ceremony before he accepted the gift. A Bauan official

was despatched to waylay a party of innocent persons to become
the substitute sacrifice for the dedication.

The scene is peaceful now. Many times I have sailed over
that very spot. When the great Wesleyan preacher Dr. W.E. Sang-
ster stayed with us at Bau, I had the pleasure of taking him
across to Viwa in a Fijian deep-sea canoe. Ashore we had a
Christian worship service between the graves of John Hunt and
Joeli Bulu, and broke the ground for a memorial chapel. I remember an idiomatic phrase from the address of welcome - not the
usual "*butuka* (walk on) our earth"; but "*vavaca*" (tread softly,
or respectfully).

Here we remembered men who had sailed in the deep-sea
canoe, who had met cannibalism and heathenism face to face, who
had sailed through hurricanes and rescued their comrades from the
oven in times of war, who took the Bible at its face value and
acted on its words - men who demonstrated their faith in action.

Nothing would be more appropriate than ending this book
at Viwa, from which the faith first spread forth in deep-sea
canoes to Bua, and Nadroga and Kadavu; where the Fijian New Testament was first printed and circulated. Two miles over the water
lies Bau, a Christian island now, where that cannibal warlord,
Cakobau, after his own conversion, built the church from the
foundations of 17 heathen temples, and turned the cannibal killing stone into a baptismal font, setting it before the generation
to follow, that they might never forget the greatness of their
salvation.

Our voyage is over. We have entered the anchorage. We
dismantle the mast. Tonight there will be a worship service in
the village and thanksgiving to God for our safe arrival. It
will then be for the young men of the island church to make the
next voyage.

General Index

Lagi, Wilisoni vii,31
Latu, Jeremaia vii
Leadership Development 69-70,
87-99
Learning from each Other 90-92
Ligeremaluonga, Osea 115
Liquor 27
Lotu, Taniela 14
Lua of Nadroga 10-11
Lyth, R.B. 92

Marau, Clement 98-99,115
Marita of Ulawa 99
Martin, Edouard 80
Masima, Ra 55
Mataika, Nacanieli 74
Mateinaniu, Josua 30-31,76,77,89
Maturity 42
Measles Epidemic in Fiji 20
Melanesian Brotherhood 1,32
Member's Tickets 82
Messenger of Peace 8,22,46
Missionary Letters, Fijian 115
Moa and *Noa* 47
Music, Fijian 73

Naceba, Fereti 73
Nasau, Mere 83-85
Naucukidi, Sailasa 38-39
Naulivou, Juliasi vii
New Guinea Highlands Movement 59
Newton, John 10
Nicholson, R.C. 116
Noa (translation assistant) 76,78

Paraphernalia, Destruction of
57-59
Patii of Eimeo 57-58
Patrick 2
Patteson, Bishop 31-32,78
Prayer of 1
Pentecostal Experience 29
[See People Movements]
People Movements 4,53-60
[See Bau, Eimeo, Kadavu, New
Guinea Highlands]
Persecution 35-40
Pilgrim's Progress 82
Pomare of Tahiti 58
Porpoise Fishing Incident 106-107

Power Encounter 42,45
"Praying Group" 62
Prevenient Grace 6f.,12
Printing in the Islands 76
Proclamation 16
Programmed Action 29,31
Providence of God 6f.,12

Qoro, Josaia 84-85

Raitea Mission 17-18
Raitilava, Josefa 73
Rarodro, Etoni 73
Ratu, Lolahea 73
Realization, Point of 42,44
Reference Bible 82
Role Creation 71
Rycroft, H.R. 116

Sapibuana, Charles 98
Salvation, Idea of 46
Seileka, Setareki 38
Sitiveni of Lasakau vii
Situation, Missionary 25-26
Situation, Penetrating the 29
Structure, Meaning of 100

Takai, Isireli 27
Taloifuila, J. 116
Tanre 9
Tatawaqa, P.E. 73
Te Deum 73
Theological Training 72,93-99
Toplady, Augustus 3
Tongan Awakening 8,19,76
Tongan Mission to Fiji 19
Tui Cakau 88-89

Varani, Ilaija 40,48-51,54,55,97
Volau, Mitiani 73
Vule, D. 116
Vuli Levu [Big School] 93

Wai of Ono 27-28
Watts, Isaac 3
Wesley, John 3,7,17
Whitefield, G. 17
Williams, F.E. 104
Williams, John 8,17-18,46,62
Williams, T. vii,54

Scripture Index

About the Author

A native of Australia, Alan R Tippett did his undergraduate work at Queen's College, Melbourne, and extramurally with the University of New Zealand. He held a Diploma in Theology (L.Th.) from the Melbourne College of Divinity, an M.A. in History from the American University, Washington, D.C., and a Ph.D. in Anthropology from the University of Oregon. Dr. Tippett was a Fellow of the Linnean Society of London and held a Hall of Nations Certificate in Archives Administration.

He served for six years as a Methodist minister in Australia, twenty years as a missionary in Fiji, and taught anthropology in Eugene, Oregon, and Pasadena, California. From 1965 to 1977 he was Senior Professor of Anthropology and Oceanic Studies at Fuller Theological Seminary, where he was engaged in missiological research in Oceania. His research took him to the British Solomon Islands, Southwest Ethiopia, Mexico, Guatemala, and the Navajo reservation.

Dr. Tippett wrote missionary reports for several supporting boards and published many articles and monographs in anthropology and in missionary history and theory. The author of seven devotional and biblical books in the Fijian language, he served as the editor of a Fijian church paper for five years. His book on the anthropology of the Fiji Islands, *Fijian Material Culture*, was published by the Bishop Museum Press, his *Solomon Islands Christianity* by Lutterworth Press (reprinted by William Carey Library in 1975), *Church Growth and the Word of God* by Eerdmans, *Peoples of Southwest Ethiopia*, *Verdict Theology in Missionary Theory*, *Aspects of Pacific Ethnohistory*, and *Introduction to Missiology* (WCL), and *People Movements of Southern Polynesia* (Moody Press), *Oral Tradition and Ethnohistory* (St Mark's Library, Canberra), William Carey Library.

In 1977, he retired to Canberra, Australia, with his library of over 16,000 books, journals and microfilms, to devote himself to research. In 1984, his library known as "The Tippett Collection" was donated to St Mark's Theological College, Canberra. From retirement until his death in 1988, he was Professor Emeritus of Fuller Seminary and Honorary Research Fellow at St Mark's Library.

Printed in the United States
46328LVS00001B/199

3 4711 00184 7237